WIELDING POWER

WIELDING POWER

The Essence of Ritual Practice

by

CHARLES R. TETWORTH

LINDISFARNE BOOKS

2002

Published by Lindisfarne Books
P.O. Box 799
Great Barrington, MA 01230
www.lindisfarne.org

Library of Congress Cataloging-in-Publication Data

Tetworth, Charles R., 1929–
    Wielding power : a practical approach to ritual / by Charles R. Tetworth.
        p. cm.
    ISBN 1-58420-006-5
    1. Magic. 2. Ritual. I. Title.
    BF1623.R6 T48 2002
    291.3'8—dc21

2001006247

Book design by STUDIO 31
WWW.STUDIO31.COM

10 9 8 7 6 5 4 3 2 1

Printed in the United States of America

Contents

FOREWORD

Z'EV BEN SHIMON HALEVI

WITH ITS INSIGHTS, EXPLANATIONS, AND WIDE VIEW OF the discipline of ritual, this work is full of riches clearly drawn from long and intimate experience with and practice of the subject.

In an ordered progression, the author presents the principles and lessons to be learned. These are deepened by reflections upon the interior and exterior forms of ritual, as well as by commentaries on the degrees and levels of conscious and unconscious modes, ranging from personal habits to cultural ceremonies. Anyone who follows the spiritual Ways of Action, Devotion, or Contemplation will find many of the exercises and meditations enlightening in their fine detail, broad viewpoint, and profound implications.

Z'ev ben Shimon Halevi is one of the world's most distinguished practitioners of the Kabbalistic tradition. His books include School of the Soul, The Way of Kabbalah, Adam and the Kabbalistic Tree, *and* Astrology and Kabbalah.

INTRODUCTION

WRITING THIS BOOK WAS NOT DIFFICULT. KNOWING what to say and what to leave unsaid, on the other hand, was not easy. No doubt I have occasionally said more than I was entitled to. However, upon me be the judgment. Those who work in the field of ritual are sometimes too jealous of their knowledge; they feel that they are the only people who practice the art. If the book shows anything, I hope it shows the reader that all human life is a ritual, self-taught and practiced by its teacher.

We all practice ritual. Some are good at it; some specialize in it; most people practice it in a general way. With a little attention our rituals can become more flexible and more effective; we might even be able to enjoy them and stop feeling guilty about using them!

There are many different practices and many different systems. But in order to illustrate the theory and practice of ritual, I have used those with which I am most familiar, even when they are not in general circulation. I do not mean to imply that these are the only methods and systems. However, they do give some idea of how ritual systems in general could be used. The methodology is fairly general but is particular to the Order of Sentinels. B.L.L. + D.A.M. + B.

I would cordially like to thank Brajangana Rai Singh for her help in writing this book.

—*Charles Raymond Tetworth*

CHAPTER ONE

RITUALS OF LIFE

Ritual requires perfected action, perfect attention, and perfect conduct. It requires the body to be disciplined, the heart to be steadfast, and the mind to be clear. Whether in Invocation, Evocation, Thankfulness, or Celebration, the purpose should be clear, the aim steady, and the power controlled. Only when these conditions are met can one be brought to that state of knowing where the unknown appears. All else is preparation, practice, and habit.

—Instructions to Members, Order of Sentinels

HUMAN BEINGS DIFFER FROM OTHER CREATURES. WE do not come into the world completely preprogrammed. We have to learn to stand, to walk, to communicate. Our knowledge of the world is not laid down in the period of gestation, ready to burst into action with the correct trigger. We program ourselves — and this makes us the most dangerous creatures on earth.

As children, we are taught to curb and control our power. We learn correct behavior and acceptable ways of using this power. We acquire information on a wide range of subjects and learn under what circumstances we can use this specialized knowledge. We as a species are not specialists with only one particular skill or faculty that has been perfected to a high degree; our abilities are generalized, so that we can apply our various skills and faculties appropriately with changing circumstances.

During the course of a day we take on various roles, for each of which we put on an appropriate mask. A doctor puts on one mask for his office, another for his fellow professionals, one for his wife, one for his children, and another when playing squash. We need to change our personae as changing circumstances require.

Ritual is one way of changing in this respect. Even in ordinary life it is necessary. Preparing to go to work, to go out with friends, for a dinner party or a sport — all of these activities require one to arrange oneself. We prepare an image and clothe it appropriately in order to present ourselves in a way that fits easily into the circumstances. This does not disqualify an eccentric who wants to stand out in a crowd: after all, even eccentrics have to spend time preparing their image!

We enact so many different rituals in so many different aspects of our everyday lives that we are scarcely aware of half of them. Just consider your day — how you use various ritualized forms of behavior to move from one circumstance to another. The repetition of these forms allows others to recognize and respond appropriately to them. Even today, despite the collapse of many socially accepted forms of behavior, people have rituals of greeting. These enable people, on meeting, to decide how they should speak to one another, what they might have in common, and where their areas of conflict might be. If you know these rituals, human interaction becomes easier.

It is said that on meeting someone, the English first look very quickly, with the most fleeting of glances, at the other person's eyes. Then their glance moves away to the chin and neck, then to the clothing, and finally to the shoes. In that rapid sequence the person is assessed. With the eyes, a very short instinctive communication takes place. The chin and neck give information not just on age, but also on attitude. The way the neck is carried gives us clues about people's attitudes: for example, we talk about "stiff-necked" people. Sometimes jewelry is worn around the neck, and that can display people's allegiances. There are more clues in the clothing a person wears: it reflects the person's subculture and the type of behavior he may be expected to conform to. And finally the shoes are assessed — whether they are fashionable, shabby, in good repair, or geared towards a specific activity.

An Italian or a Frenchman will have a different ritual for greeting and assessing the person. Each country has its own ritual, and sometimes these rituals differ from region to region even within the country. The purpose remains the same, however. It is a means of easing interaction and establishing a relationship within the framework of the social structure and culture. That is why many people carry badges as a means of speeding up such a process — an old school tie, a crucifix, a slave chain on the ankle, a ban-the-bomb symbol. By such means, members of subgroups identify one another. They have also evolved rituals of behavior that they all share and understand, so that they know the right sequence to follow in the pursuit of business, courting, challenge and submission, eating, or leisure.

Most of what has just been described could be seen as purely habitual. Indeed it is true that each part of a ritual is habitual — on meeting someone, you automatically say "hello" — but a ritual is more than that; it is a series of habitual or learned patterns connected together in a definite sequence. This weaving together in a sequential and ordered manner turns haphazard habits, which are simply nonvolitional responses to a trigger, into a ritual. Even in the animal kingdom the mating, defending, or challenging processes are ritualistic and form a sequence of steps.

Each step in the sequence also has built within it an opportunity to break the pattern and stop the encounter from continuing. At every step, there is the chance to advance, retreat, or start a new sequence. In the animal world, rituals control the most important aspects of life, such as courtship, mating, and position in the pecking order. This is also true in the case of social animals, since one can challenge for leadership in the hierarchy. These rituals control drives that are basic to all living creatures. In many cases they control the survival instinct, because the possibility of the ritual moving into a "live-or-die" situation does happen in certain species. But if there were no built-in provision within the sequence for one creature to submit to the superior force of another, the species would soon die out.

In the world of the human animal as well there are rituals of aggression with steps at which the sequence can be broken off. Take the following example. The scene is a pub. Two men catch each other's eyes.

> **A:** "What are you looking at then?" (Here is an opportunity for the other person to apologize.)
> **B:** "I was looking at you." (He takes up the challenge.)
> **A:** "Look elsewhere then." (An opportunity to break off.)
> **B:** "I'll look where I like." (Continuing the challenge.)
> **A:** "You watch out!" (Still giving room to back off.)
> **B:** "Says who?" (Still challenging.)
> **A:** "I do!" (Picking up the challenge at last.)
> **B:** "Who the hell do you think you are?" (Now the final steps of the challenge begin.)
> **A:** "I'll show you who I am." (Threats at last!)
> **B:** "Yeah! You and whose army?" (Battle is now inevitable.)

A: "Outside." (What this means precisely depends on the rules of battle that prevail in the area: it could involve a battle with bottles, glasses, razors, knives, or just plain fists.)
B: "Make me." (He has to fight now.)

Everyone in the pub has by now become aware of the clash, and the other men now push them out into the open if the battle is to be formal. In certain parts of the country the battle breaks out immediately on the premises.

Of course, the real reason for starting the sequence is some imagined slight, to display manhood before a girl-friend, or to establish superiority within a group. There are many different reasons for starting the aggressive sequence, and there are as many different arenas in which this ritual of aggression can take place. The reasons may vary, but the ritual sequence itself is very similar to the process of the leader of a pack of animals being challenged by another who is attempting to rise higher in the pecking order.

Rituals need to be appropriate to the circumstances, and the people taking part in them need to understand the same things by the same actions. During World War II, many American servicemen were stationed in England. Naturally they wanted to meet English girls, and just as naturally the English girls wanted to meet them. After a short time, the girls considered the Americans immoral and their reputation among the English began to deteriorate. The GIs also began to feel contemptuous of the ladies. The situation got so bad that a team of U.S. Army psychologists was brought in to investigate it. The problem arose out of the different courting rituals of the two countries, and the solution was not an easy one. In America, probably originally because of a shortage of women, it had become traditional during courtship for women to be responsible for calling a halt to the development of a relationship. For the English girls, the opposite held true: they expected the men to stop things from going too far. As they did not share a common understanding of the courtship ritual, relationships moved far too fast; both the men and the women were dissatisfied, with each convinced that the other side was to blame. To solve the problem it was necessary to start an educational program to inform the American GIs about English ways.

MARKING LIFE CHANGES

Among the many rituals we have evolved in our everyday lives, there are those that have arisen to mark the life cycle of a human being. In the process of life, from the first breath to the last, the human being grows and dies. In this long process there are specific ages that mark turning points in growth, and we have evolved rituals around these points, both to empower their significance and to ease the transition into the next phase of life. There are four great ritual points in life that are the most fundamental. These four have been acknowledged by all people in all times and will probably continue to be acknowledged in the future too, because they reflect human nature.

The first point is the actual birth of a child. This has its rituals, whether it is the modern shower party in the U.S., which prepares for the birth, the particular rites in the actual birthing, or religious purificatory rites for the mother after the birth. In most societies, these rituals are purely the business of the women.

The next point for ritual is the naming of the child. This is a very important step because it focuses the child's identity, which is already recognizable by others. In Christian societies the ritual is conducted within a religious context, so that the child is both formally named and publicly acknowledged as a new member of the Church. Others besides the parents take on moral and spiritual duties with regard to the child, and these godparents also name the child. In the baptismal ceremony, the priest blesses the child, ensures that the godparents are in a fit state to take on their new responsibilities, confirms the name by wetting the child's forehead and in some cases anointing the child with holy oil. Finally the congregation receives the child as a new member of the Church.

The next major ritual in life is that of marriage. This, of course, is preceded by courtship, which has its own rituals, but in the act of marriage the bringing together of two people becomes a matter of public concern. Even in a purely secular society there is a ceremony conducted by an official of the state in front of a witness. In religious societies, it is a major rite calling upon the clergy to exercise their priestly role. In many cultures, it is not a matter of just two individuals starting a new life but two families creating new bonds. Sometimes this is seen purely in terms of material gain (the old dowry system), while at others it is more a recognition of different bloodlines being connected. Whatever the motives, marriage is on the whole a celebratory affair, calling forth all the pomp and splendor of which people are capable.

The fourth and final major ritual in life is that of death. Here the ritual takes the form of burial or cremation; even in societies where death rites have lost their importance, the death is still registered in public records. In most societies, rituals surrounding death involve a eulogy and a recognition of those qualities by which the person will be remembered by friends and acquaintances. There is a public display of either grief or rejoicing, depending on the views held about the afterlife.

Apart from these four main junctures in life, some

cultures also ritually emphasize the importance of children reaching the age of responsibility. The age at which this is acknowledged depends on the cultural view, but it is again a public ceremony, which stresses the taking up of responsibilities and becoming a participating member of a tribe or society. In Judaism, it is marked by the bar mitzvah. At the age of thirteen, a boy is considered to be responsible, and he is called from the congregation to read from the Book of Law. In some societies at the same age, boys are circumcised as their mark of reaching manhood.

Some cultures also mark the first menstruation of a girl, but acknowledgment of this is usually restricted to the women themselves. In cultures where this is done, the sexes are organized separately for their rites of passage and the boys too have their male mysteries, which the women must never see.

OTHER COMMON RITUALS

The passage of the year is frequently marked by rituals that acknowledge the rhythm to which all people are subject and attempt to help people live in accord with the swing of life. Originally these rituals arose within a simpler, agricultural way of life. The four turning points of the year were marked: springtime for the first planting, summer as the period of growth, autumn for the fruits of labor, and winter as a time of gestation. These four points usually coincide with the equinoxes and solstices — the spring equinox, when day and night are of equal length; the summer solstice, when the daylight hours are longest; the autumn equinox, when day and night are again of equal length; the winter solstice, when the hours of daylight are shortest.

There also arose rituals to mark the appearance and disappearance of the moon, recognizing the shorter cycle of the moon within the larger cycle of the year. The moon's position in the sky can be fixed against the backdrop of the fixed stars, and so it can be used to mark the passage of time and as a basis for an annual calendar. Even today, religions and societies that originated in the cloudless band of the equator or in desert areas, such as Islam, Judaism, and Buddhism, pay particular attention to the new moon.

In some cultures of old, probably those that hunted by night, the rising of certain stars became important. Other celestial phenomena that became targets for rituals were eclipses, both of the sun and of the moon. The dramatic disappearance of the sun could well cause fright and disturbance, and many rituals used noise to drive away the beast that appears to be eating away the sun or the moon. In some areas the spectacular appearance of meteors was also celebrated.

Then there are rituals that display allegiance and power. The great May Day parades of the former Eastern Bloc, the Independence Day celebrations in the U.S., the Queen's Birthday Parade in Britain, Bastille Day in France — all these are concerned with the people of a nation publicly displaying who and what they are. In a more solemn and valedictory mood, we also commemorate the dead of our nations. All these great rituals have the power to move us by evoking within us the appropriate responses.

RELIGION AND MAGIC

So far little has been said about the rituals of religion. Those who have been brought up in a religion will be aware of its rituals, but their significance may be unclear. In many religions the rituals have been added to over the course of centuries, until the original meanings and purposes have been lost or obscured. In many cases the participants perform their parts without having the slightest idea of what they are actually doing. This is often because the "specialists" in ritual — the priests and acolytes — have taken over the duties and responsibilities of the participants. However, if people are to participate actively in a ritual, they need to be aware of the significance of every single part of it; otherwise it is as mechanical and meaningless as putting a coin in a slot machine, pressing the right buttons, and letting a record play.

Although our response to the record is also often automatic, at other times we do appreciate its beauty. It does have meaning. The problem for the ritualist is how a familiar sequence of actions can retain purpose and meaning. Knowledge is the prerequisite for this. If the people performing the actions know what they are doing, then, even when a participant does not understand every single part of the sequence, rituals can at least be comforting. In times of trouble, old and familar rituals are very sustaining, like a warm blanket on a cold and merciless night. They allow you to face the shocks in life and prepare you to meet the unknown. In contrast, habitual actions and responses save you the trouble of thinking or feeling in any depth, and so are not genuinely sustaining.

Rituals have evolved within all religious traditions. Those traditions with a historical founder, like Jesus Christ, Mohammed, or Buddha, have rituals that focus around the main events in the founder's life. Each event is ritually and liturgically enacted. Of course, as a tradition evolves it also incorporates within its life other great beings — martyrs, saints, teachers, prophets, mystics — who have upheld and extended the work of the founder, and they are duly remembered, called upon, and commemorated. This cycle of events then becomes the basis of the calendar, and by ritually reliving these events year in and year out, the followers become part of the rhythm of the tradition and in time conform to the being of the founder. Anybody who takes their religion seriously will witness to the changes in their being, life, and knowledge that their religion reveals. Everybody knows that Christianity is not just about going to church on Sundays, that Islam is not just about taking the prayer mat out five times a day, and that Buddhism is not just about rattling the oracle sticks. If ritual loses its meaning and significance for the followers, it often degenerates into empty observance. But ritual is a means that all religions use to affect the participants in every aspect of their lives, so that they conform to the divine manifestation they are celebrating.

In Hinduism, where God is glorified in all His manifestations, the forms of worship that arise are manifold. Whether they celebrate the incarnation in Lord Krishna and enact his life cycle or see God in a blade of grass, the diversity of forms is held together by a common socioreligious structure. This is the hierarchical fourfold caste system. The priests, rulers, traders, and workers have strictly prescribed functions and rules of conduct. The system itself is a model of order and ritual.

In Judaism every action performed is dedicated to God. Indeed every part of the human body is dedicated to God. The whole emphasis is on ritual purity, and everything is categorized as clean or unclean. All actions performed — from cleaning a cup to sexual behavior — are done according to formulae intended to remind the participant of the Divine Presence.

Confucianism has developed ritual to a fine art. Every relationship is a matter of ritual. Its fundamental belief, like that of other so-called "nature" religions, is that everything is alive and has a spirit that has power for good or evil. So it is very important to Confucians that everything is given due importance according to its nature. One might suppose that the "natural" life is very simple. This is not so. The winds, the trees, the rivers, the streams, the rocks and mountains, the plants and animals all have life and intelligence, and their relationship to each other is complicated. They are also able to exert their influence on people. Far from being simple, it is a complex process whereby one is required to treat each being according to its nature, and to take great care not to upset these beings. So rituals are created to ensure that the correct attitude and relationship is maintained with these beings.

In Taoism, where everything is perceived as a constantly moving balance between yin and yang, one might suppose that no rituals would be necessary. However, if it is perceived that there is, within a situation, an imbalance between yin and yang, with one predominating to the detriment of the whole organism, it becomes necessary to correct the balance. Acupuncture and dietary practices can be counted among the rituals of Taoism, each having the purpose of correcting these imbalances and maintaining a proper balance.

Shamanism can be seen as a form of animism. However, the prime element in shamanism is magical rather than religious, because the shaman has to gain mastery of the spirits. The shaman's training is extremely rigorous and many would-be shamans die in the process of empowerment. In order to obtain mastery, the shaman has to lose much of what anchors a person to ordinary life and meet powers and forces that are terrifying in their aspects. The shaman must venture forth into the world of the biosphere, with all its history of dinosaurs, teeming hordes of insects, dog packs, tigers, eagles, earthquakes, and volcanoes, and deal with their power. Such a world is very, very dangerous, as any competent psychologist will tell you. It is truly a descent into the ravening hell of the id. To be able to encounter this world, the shaman's training has to be very severe.

In a way, the function of ritual within shamanism shows the importance of ritual in general. Ritual provides the base and foundation from which the shaman can step out into the unknown. Most importantly, it serves as a familiar base to return to after venturing into the world of the biosphere. Usually this base takes the form of a trance, and developing that trance state takes years of practice.

It is difficult to separate magical ritual methods and common religious practices. Each has elements of the other, and in many ways to separate them is to create an artificial division that takes away from rather than adds to our understanding of either. The shamanic journey is a religious quest; the Catholic Mass contains elements that are common to magic. The water with which members of the congregation cross themselves as they enter the church is empowered by a ritual of blessing. However, if we begin by distinguishing the basic elements in all ritual, irrespective of whether they belong to a magical or a religious tradition, we might gain some insight into the nature of ritual itself.

In any magical or religious ritual, three main elements may be discerned. First, there is invocation, where the power of saints, angels, or prophets, the power of the teacher or messenger, or the power of the Lord Himself is called down. Second, there is evocation, where a desired state in both the priests and celebrants is brought into being through prayer or repeated activities. Third, there is participation, in which the form brings together the Divine and the individual. Different kinds of ritual are employed for each of these three elements. A particular ritual might be devoted to just one of the three elements, or it may involve a combination of two or all three of them.

The Varieties of Ritual

Defense

Rituals are conducted within a space — an external space that should be mirrored by an internal space within the ritualist. We define a space by giving it certain limits. Your garden fence denotes the limits of your private space, and your behavior is modified by which side of the fence you are on. After all, what you do inside your house is very different from what you can do outside it. Defense rituals, which are primarily of an invocatory nature, are a means of creating and maintaining a suitable space in which a ritual can take place. This is done by excluding extraneous influences or by including influences that are in accord with the general purpose of the ritual. Typical methods for excluding alien influences are the delineation of the space by sprinkling charged or holy water, by surrounding it with fire or with the scents of herbs and spices, or by chanting sacred texts. One can call upon the powers of angels or good influences to act as guardians of the space. Patron saints act as guardians of churches and people.

Commemoration

This is an act of remembrance in which all relevant matters are brought to mind. By reading prayers and scriptures, or by the remembrance of past events recorded in sacred books, or by recalling great figures who embodied particular qualities, all the relevant associations are triggered, invoked, and enlivened. This evokes in the participants the qualities desired for the operation. Identification with archetypal beings or events recreates the desired attitude in the mind and being of the participant. Commemoration can form only a part of a ritual, as in many religious services, or it can be the whole ritual (whether religious, magical, or secular). It can be a celebratory thanksgiving.

Initiation

Initiation is a beginning; it is the first step. Intuitively we know that the first step we take, when making or starting something new, is important and colors the whole event. How you get up in the morning can determine the pattern of the day. How you start off a new relationship can set the tone for a lifetime. Initiation rituals therefore seek to enhance the power of beginnings. Where religions are concerned, there is always some form of initiation. In Judaism, it is the circumcision of the male, which is performed when he is at the most eight days old, so that the event is remembered at a nonverbal level. Child baptism is the norm in the Christian Church today, and this too is performed at an age where it is lodged in a child at a nonverbal level. In some Christian sects, the baptism is an imitation of Christ's baptism by John and is undertaken by adults so that the initiation is received in full consciousness.

Within the magical tradition, people to be initiated are brought to a position where they can be shown that they are about to start on what may be a lengthy journey. They are usually asked about their motivation, their faith, and their willingness to commit themselves to the journey. Often an oath of allegiance is taken, and the consequences of breaking that oath are also made known. The oath itself is something that cannot be talked about freely. Recently there has been much criticism surrounding this question of oaths, but it is extremely useful for the individual to have made such a commitment. The element of secrecy enables the person to keep a guard on his or her tongue and helps to build strength and self-discipline. It is a means of conserving the creative power within. Most creative artists are aware that if they talk about what they want to do, the impetus runs away. It is as if the power that should go into the creative process itself has gone into the process of speech, and its manifestation in that form has left little power for the actual creation. Secret oaths of allegiance are a means of helping initiates to keep to their chosen path.

Empowerment

By means of these rituals, the person who receives an object or substance that has been empowered is enabled to embody that power. By invoking the Trinity, the Catholic Church empowers the bread and wine and transubstantiates it into the very presence of Jesus Christ. The priests and congregation then embody the Divine Person in a participatory ritual. In the old knightly rituals, the sword and spear were dedicated to an objective, and the appropriate power was invoked and made to flow into them. It was as if they contained this power. Sometimes this process is called "charging." It can be likened to the process of building up a static charge on glass by rubbing it with a silk cloth. Or perhaps you have seen, in laboratories, the large metal balls that store electrons; the charge builds up and flashes over like lightning from one ball to another. If the receiver of the charge is weak and cannot contain the huge flow of electricity, it is damaged.

This illustrates one problem with empowerment. What is being charged or empowered has to be capable of holding that charge without breaking down itself or damaging other things around it. On a small scale, one can see this when a person who cannot handle power is given power over others. He either burns himself out or he is taken over by the power of the position and loses all sense of proportion. For this reason, no one should be empowered unless he or she is capable of receiving that power. If they are capable of receiving and handling power, they actually grow in stature with the authority vested in them and dispense power in the appropriate manner. It is not power itself that is corrupting; power is merely a means of doing something.

Power is certainly dangerous, but without it how can anything be achieved? Water collected and stored is potentially dangerous: if a dam's walls burst, for instance, then it can cause a great deal of havoc. If contained water is released through a controlled channel, it can generate power and that power may be dangerous; if it is released in such small quantities that it is not dangerous, it is also no longer a source of energy. Every time we turn on our taps, we use that source of power. We are able to do something with the water. It is useful. Empowerment, therefore, is the harnessing of energy and releasing it through a controlled channel into a receiver capable of storing and utilizing it.

Confirmation

This requires individuals to demonstrate both to themselves and others that they do indeed have the power, ability, or status conferred upon them. What may have been a temporary state of affairs is confirmed as a fact. For example, in the services, in times of war, people are promoted to an "acting rank" by the need of the situation itself in order to fulfill a particular function. This is a temporary status, which can either be removed once the function is fulfilled, or it might be recognized that the temporary state had now become permanent. Within the magical tradition, a person may be initiated and empowered to carry out certain functions. The fulfilling of the function evokes the desired state of being in the person that is finally confirmed in some manner. Within the Christian Church, the individual is initiated at baptism and, on reaching the age of discretion, is brought through teaching and practice to a state where he is capable of taking over the responsibilities which had previously been in the charge of the godparents, and is confirmed in this by the laying on of hands.

Discovery

A distinction may be made between divination and discovery. While discovery is the uncovering of what already exists, divination is the intuition of what may happen in the future (see the section on divination below). Among the Theosophists and some sects of the magical tradition, it is said that whatever has existed leaves traces in the present world. These traces exist, as matter is said to exist, in the akashic records. This rather tenuous level of existence is supposed to be capable of exploration.

Perhaps this principle can be discerned in a theory of reincarnation. If a being lives and dies, that life has left its trace within the history of the human species. If the being is reborn, lives another life, and dies, that too is recorded — and so on, with everyone who ever has been and will be. The traces of all these lives persist at that tenuous level of existence within the psyche of the species, and it would be this level that would need to be explored.

How could this be done? Imagine that our genetic inheritance is a tree with many branches, and that we stand at the end of a branch as leaf, flower, bud, or fruit. If we travel back along our genetic branch and reach a point where another branch joins it, then we might be able to transfer to that other branch and travel along it, and so on.

To travel in this way requires a splitting off of a portion of consciousness and sending it by some means along the branches of the tree. Extending the image further, we can say that in this way it might be possible to identify with any being who had lived in the past. However, there are dangers in this, not the least of which is that the people who leave the strongest traces in the human psyche and have had most effect on their descendants are the ones who are most easily identified with; one's consciousness can thus be absorbed into that identity. That way lies madness.

Another working principle here is that all existence exists in the present moment, and everything is contained in everything else after its own manner. So whatever exists now also exists within our own selves, and by accessing that within ourselves we can become aware of what is happening in another space-time continuum.

The difficulty here, as with other experiences, is that this kind of awareness of what is happening elsewhere is nonverbal and nonconceptual. I do not speak Russian. If I became aware of what is happening in Russia, all I could experience would be the feeling of being Russian. None of the labels that I have acquired in my life coincide with Russian labels and concepts, and my description of the experience would be limited to my conditioning. So the nonverbal experience has to pass through one's acquired system of images and words.

We are not, therefore, dealing here with the transference of thoughts or images (incidentally, there is enough modern evidence to show that thought transference does not work), but rather with states that can be felt and which are then translated into one's own conceptual framework. There are many well-authenticated cases in which people whose beings are strongly linked, such as identical twins, can affect one another at a distance. It is strong and definite changes in states of being that are transmittable and receivable by some people.

The ritual required for discovery, then, must be capable of evoking a specific state of being that can be explored. It does not consist of imagining another person, but of *being* the other person and feeling the changes that occur in one's being, and then attempting to translate the meanings of such changes into one's own system of words and images.

Sacrifice

Business circles appreciate the well-known occult maxim that there is no such thing as a free lunch! You pay for everything. If you want something badly enough, you can get it, but you have to be willing to pay for it. If you wish to enter the world of the spirit, you will have to give up the rewards of the material world. Justice or karma is the operating law. If you wish to achieve divine union, you must necessarily give up your own will. The things you personally value most must be sacrificed for the sake of things of greater value. In Christianity, Jesus made the supreme sacrifice for the benefit of mankind. Buddha sacrificed his royalty, his family, and possessions and even that which all hold dear, himself, in order to attain nirvana. He then sacrificed the freedom of nirvana by returning to teach the world a method of release from suffering.

Divination

We probably think of divination as a way of foretelling the future by reading omens and signs, and in the West these activities have certainly moved away from the sphere of the sacred. We no longer have anything like the oracle of Delphi. Horoscopes in the daily newspaper do not quite have the same ring to them!

Divination literally means becoming one with the divine. The purpose of divinatory rituals is to bring about in individuals a state of knowledge and being that allows them to become one with the divine within them. It is from this basis that they can know the creative possibilities inherent in each moment and in each being, and this is done by using the divine within oneself to know the divine within the other being. The divine within becomes one with the divine in the other, and in this union there is knowledge. It is a sublime knowledge. It is seeing for oneself. This may or may not be expressible. Sometimes the image of what is seen is taken to be the truth itself rather than a clothing of what is present. If the imagery has any objective resonance, then what is seen can be communicated to others. On the other hand, sometimes what is seen is inexpressible. As St. Paul said, "And I knew such a man (whether in the body, or out of the body, I cannot tell: God knoweth;) how that he was caught up into paradise, and heard unspeakable words, which it is not lawful for a man to utter" (2 Cor. 12:3–4).

— CHAPTER TWO —

PREPARING THE GROUND

Do not bring the dust of the world into this space.
It is holy: it is the Temple of the Lords and Ladies.
The work is difficult enough without further com-
plications. Simplify, simplify, simplify.

—Instructions to Members, Order of Sentinels

WHEN YOU INVITE A PERSON TO DINNER, YOU KNOW you will have to clean the place and think about the menu and how you will entertain them. You choose the food, the drink, the entertainment, all within the limits of your budget. You pay attention to the atmosphere of the room and create the right ambience by arranging flowers or changing the lighting or whatever it takes. If you decide to hold a dinner party, the task becomes even more complex, because you have the problem — fascinating though it may be — of getting the right mix of people. Many hours of careful planning and preparation may well be involved. And that is before the party has even started. As host or hostess, you still have the task of supervising the whole party: you have to effect the introductions, arrange the entertainment, and make sure that the food arrives hot at the right time and that guests are not neglected. You keep an eye on all the interchanges between the guests, drawing out the shy ones, and controlling the exuberance of the extraverts so that they give others a chance. It is only when the last guest departs that you can truly relax, and even then you have the task of returning the place back to normal. You have enacted a ritual.

Like the dinner party, a ritual requires careful planning and deliberation. The aim has to be clear so that the plans are appropriate. There is not much point in bringing out the silver and crystal if it is a party for children. The aim modifies the arrangements and sets the context and pattern of the whole ritual. So it is extremely important that everything should be conducive to the aim, and care has to be taken that random factors that could adversely affect the proceedings are reduced to a minimum. A high degree of discrimination is required to make clear distinctions between what arrangements are or are not relevant to the aim of the ritual. In alchemy this process of differentiation is called *separatio et conjunctio* — "separation and combination." Without the necessary separation, there can be no new combination, no genuinely new event: the ritual will either conform to the prior categories or expectations of the participants, or will simply become an unrecognizable mishmash.

The first thing to ensure is that the physical space to be used is suitable for ritual activities. A space must be set aside. In our homes, rooms are defined by what we do in them, and we try to keep the various functions separate, as this helps us to pursue those activities. It would be impractical to have a gym in your dining room or allow ball games in a library. In the same way, the space for ritual work should be free from extraneous activities. It is true that many Masonic Temples are in pubs, but where this is so, the publican usually does not let the room out for any other purpose. In modern America, Christian church services are sometimes held on the beach, but the Eucharist does not have quite the same impact when you are repelling flies and getting the sand out of your shoes. Here the possibility of random factors entering the ritual space have been multiplied a hundredfold.

THE ELEMENTS

Once a suitable place has been set aside, its cleanliness is the next factor to be tackled. In the field of ritual, a space is clean if it is free of dirt, corruption, and external interferences on every level. The levels on which these external interferences can occur are symbolized by four worlds or degrees of organization.

The first level is the world of substance and structure. It is our "familiar" world of materiality. I put "familiar" in quotes, because we usually only recognize the outer shapes of material things, whereas they consist of far more than their outer appearances. The underlying structure is less easily perceived, but it is what gives things their substance and independent physical existence. We symbolize this level — the totality of outer form and inner structure — as EARTH.

The next level is the world of flow. The necessary condition for flow is polarity: between the extremes of each pole there is established a movement and a constant process of evening out. This creates perceptible patterns. At this level we are concerned with all manners of flow — the flow between people, for example, like that between husband and wife or between buyer and seller. There are also flows created by the interaction of a culture and an individual, as a culture conditions the behavior pattern of an individual, and in turn the individual can add to the cultural heritage by what he or she does. Flows of course also exist in any matter that has polarized by heat, for example. A city such as London has its flows: imagine it as a vast psychic pool, with waves, whirlpools, and disturbances. This level is best symbolized by WATER.

Sometimes in a city a sudden change occurs; flashing out from its source, it affects everyone in the vicinity. The start of a parade or a marathon can suddenly disrupt a particular section of the city by creating traffic jams and delays, and it can cause a sudden buzz of excitement, felt by everyone within its sphere of influence — then, just as suddenly, it is all over and things return to normal. Sudden appearance and disappearance are the basic characteristic of the third level. These changes do not flow, but like the switching on of a light, they are suddenly there or suddenly gone. This level is concerned with energy itself. In ourselves, its mode of operation can be perceived in the experience of enthusiasm, for example, with its sudden bursts of energy. This level is symbolized by FIRE.

There is also a level that encompasses the previous three levels. It can be seen as all the necessary conditions or circumstances where earth, water, and fire can operate and thus deals with the creation of a field that is apt for the purpose. We could call it space, but it is commonly called AIR.

CLEARING THE SPACE

In preparing a space or a room for the operation of a ritual, cleaning has to be undertaken on each of the four levels. This is done by appropriate use of the four elements. You should be simply dressed in a clean bathrobe or overalls for the purpose. Some people use elaborate robes, but these are not necessary. Apart from the actual dusting and sweeping of a room, it is also important to dissipate the remains of any strong states of being that linger in the room and do not aid the particular purpose of the ritual. We do this through the operation of sound. Nearly everyone, on entering an old building, has experienced the feeling that it is full of ghosts.

These ghosts are not normally perceptible and may in fact only exist in one's mind; nevertheless one can often sense an almost palpable atmosphere of the building's past. Normally, when people move into a new home, as a matter of some urgency, they redecorate or refurnish the place. If it is already furnished, they move the furniture around and change the surroundings. They make a lot of bustle and noise and gradually they begin to put their own stamp on the place and start to feel "at home." By these methods we loosen the influence of the past and make a space our own.

Ritually, one way of dissipating any influences present in a room or building that may have been used for different purposes is to make a great deal of random noise. A traditional way of doing this is to take two large stones and strike them together randomly while walking all the way round the walls. The place should be empty. As one strikes the stones together, one becomes aware of the features of the room or building — its height, length, and breadth — and any intrinsic feel it may have. One becomes aware of the field of the room or building. As the process of striking the stones continues, that field begins to weaken, and gradually your field, or at least what you recognize as yours, begins to predominate. At this point you start to strike the stones in a more rhythmic pattern, one with which you feel at home. Continue with this rhythm until you feel you know the sound of the place.

The next stage in the process of cleansing the room for ritual use involves water. You will need water that has been charged; Christians should use holy water. If charged or holy water cannot be obtained, then rainwater that has been collected in a brand-new container may be used. On the other hand, if you are in the country, it is usually simple to collect water from a spring or a hill stream that is above the level of the place you are in. Water from a well should not be used. Taking this clear or charged water, it is then necessary to go round the building sprinkling the walls with a new brush dipped in the water. Don't forget the floor and ceilings!

Next comes fire. For this you need good, dry wood that burns with a clear flame. Pine can be used, but make sure that it is not a smoky pine. Beeswax candles or stalks of dry yarrow are good as well. Many Americans like to use sage wands. Take your flame all around the walls and corners of the room. There is little risk of damage; after all, you still have the water to hand. Fire is often combined with air by using incense or scented wood. This is fine if the building has already been used for the same ritual purpose you are planning to use it for, but it is not sufficient if you are starting from scratch.

The last stage in the process starts with creating a draft of air through the room. Next, put some herbs — marjoram, thyme, rosemary, lavender, pine needles — in a wide pottery plate and heat the plate so that the scents are liberated. Be careful not to use too strong a scent, and do not use scents bought from a shop.

With this, the cleaning of the ritual space is now finished. You do not need to have complete belief in what you are doing. What is required is an attitude of open-mindedness and an ability to keep the whole room or building in mind; that is to say, your vision should be as wide as possible and all your senses should be alert. You should keep your attention on what you are doing in a light but serious manner. Having cleansed the space of previous influences by sound, water, fire, and scent, remove all the things that have been used from the room. Now you have completed your spring cleaning.

SEALING THE SPACE

The next stage of the process is called "sealing the space." This is to ensure that no extraneous influences can enter the cleared space. For this we invite guests who are supposed to have dominion over certain realms to act as guardians of the working space. We may think of these entities as archetypal forces, as a hierarchy of angels and archangels, or as the vast pantheon of gods and goddesses that human beings in all times and places have perceived. Whatever we may conceive them to be, they are within common human experience and have meaning for us. These entities may well have an objective reality. But we are not required to believe or agree on their form of existence. They exist within us if they have been meditated with, pondered upon, and thought about until they acquire distinctive characteristics. This enables us to recognize their various qualities, and to know which principles each of them conform to and what areas of experience they relate to, so that they can be arranged in a proper configuration within oneself.

For each stage of a ritual to be appropriately formed, we need to be clear about its overall purpose. Having decided the purpose, then, we can invite the appropriate guests to guard the ritual space. For this I shall now turn to the Order of Sentinels' Workbook. The entities described there have their equivalents in the Greco-Roman tradition, so I shall use these names, because they may be more familiar. There are the Lord and Lady who have dominion over all that conforms to the principle of light, as do Zeus, or Jupiter, and Hera, or Juno. There are the Lord and Lady of the Waters, who may be known as Poseidon or Neptune, and Demeter or Ceres. Then there are the Lord and Lady who have dominion over the fields of space, as do Hades or

Dis or Pluto, and Hestia or Vesta. These are the guests who
are invited and, as at a dinner party, they must be acknowledged and welcomed in a fitting manner. After all, if you
invite guests to a dinner party and are offhand with them,
they will react accordingly, and your party already has the
seeds of difficulty sown within it. To welcome these guests,
you must know what seats of honor they are to occupy, and
for this the purpose of the ritual must be clear.

So we must clarify the purpose of the ritual. Is it to be
concerned with appearances, visions, or images? If it is,
then the matter comes under the powers of the Lord and
Lady of Light. Therefore the *guardians* of the space must be
the Lord and Lady of the Waters and the Lord and Lady of
the Fields of Space. Or is the purpose of the ritual the
changing of conditions or of the ground where things may
occur? In this case, the Lord and Lady of the Fields of Space
are the *rulers* and the other two pairs of Lords and Ladies
become the *guardians*. Or, finally, is the ritual concerned
with the flow of power, either in emanation or in reception?
If it is, then the Lord and Lady of the Waters are the rulers
and the other two pairs can act as the guardians.

Suppose we have chosen a ceremony whose object is to
awaken within the participants an image of the Light. We
must now greet our guards:

> "Lady of the Fields, of the fields under the fields,
> of the fields over the fields, you who guard the flame
> that sprang from under the earth, and the flame that
> springs from over the earth, we pray you, be the
> guardian of this ritual in the east.
>
> "Lord of the Fields, lord of the world under the
> world, lord of the world above the world, you who
> break the mountains, empty lakes, bury men and bring

them to serve the art of life, we humbly beseech you to guard the west.

"Lord of the Waters, you who bring the waves, who stir the waters of the earth, the waters of heaven and the waters of the starry sky, who turns the planets in their courses, stand, we beseech you, in the north and guard our purpose.

"Lady of the Waters, the healing waters, the gift of the heavens, the bringer of seeds, the lady of harvests, the blood of all living which flows in the earth, above the earth, even unto the starry heavens, we humbly request you to stand guard in the south."

You should now look at the places in the room — into the east, the south, the north and the west — and see the guardians' images in your mind's eye: they stand there winged, as all great beings are. See them standing, with their wings outstretched and wingtips just touching. You have completed the task of setting up the guardians, who have, in effect, created secure, imperceptible walls.

It only remains to fill the floor and the ceiling of the work space. For this you need to call upon the Lord and Lady under whose rulership the ritual is being undertaken and to work out which is above and which is below. If you recall, the object of this ritual was to awaken an image of the Light within the participants; the participants, therefore, are the receivers of the light. The Lady of Light is the receiver of light and the Lord of Light causes the light to appear. So we set the receiver first below, by evoking the correct state within the participants:

"Lady of Light, by whom all appearances are nurtured; Lady of Light, light of the moon, light of the sun, light of the heavens, awaken in our minds and hearts the desire to see." That which causes the light to appear must then be invoked: "Lord of Light, great lord of the stars themselves, lord of the sun in splendor, master of all skills, you of the golden bow, let your light shine on us, we pray you."

Now you have set all the conditions for the ritual to take place. The conditions are not the ritual itself, for that may follow different patterns — the patterns of the great artisans and workers that take the form of initiation, reception, growth, limitation, transformation, and performance. For the moment, you are still preparing the space in which these may occur.

PREPARING THE INSTRUMENTS

All rituals require tools through which the purpose or aim is effected. Following the alchemical principle of *separatio et conjunctio*, it is impossible to operate successfully unless there is a clear distinction made between different principles and functions. So we create symbolic instruments to help us accomplish this. Among the usual instruments used in ritual work are knives, swords, spears, cups or bowls, cards and cloths, aprons and robes, altars, and stones. Each is used in a specific manner: you do not cut with a stone, nor do you use a blunt knife if you want to chop your vegetables efficiently. These instruments have to be cared for and maintained so that the best use can be made of them. Ritual instruments that have been in storage must be cleaned and discharged of any unwanted characteristics they may have acquired. Some instruments are used only occasionally; these should be stored with care. When the instruments are taken out of storage, they should be named for their qualities and an appropriate dedication should be spoken over them. The instruments should be purified — that is, cleaned, washed, passed through the flame, and dried out in the air.

In the world of the Parsi, the Muslim, the Jew, and the Hindu many things are considered to be ritually clean or unclean, and the process of purification has sometimes been taken to extremes. Physical purity has become part of the religious observances of these traditions and has acquired a symbolic meaning to create a greater awareness of the sacred in everyday life. This may well lead to physical perfection of a kind, but that was never the intention of the rules. The alchemical principle of *separatio et conjunctio* should again be recalled. One could, I suppose, carry out a successful business transaction while washing the baby's bottom, but it would make each task more difficult!

THE PREPARATION WITHIN

Preparing one's inner ground is just as important as preparing the outer space. What use is having fixed the purity of the outer circumstances, if one is confused and idly repeating meaningless phrases to oneself? A great deal of inner work has to take place. If feelings of anger, envy, greed, sloth, jealousy, possessiveness, or depression affect one's attitude to the work, there is little chance of success. If this work is undertaken for reasons of revenge or ambition, it will only write one's faults larger. Therefore the task of clearing one's internal ground is important. A good maxim for this is: "No regrets. What has passed has passed, so let us begin again." But we each have a personal history, and at any given moment we are a consequence of all our characteristics, both good and bad. We have our conditioning, our feelings and thoughts that are peculiar to us and which arise with alarming familiarity in different circumstances. Every time we give vent to our favorite bad feeling or respond in the same old way, we fortify them by repeating them. To be able to put aside the past and to begin afresh, without feelings of guilt or remorse, we have to cultivate the faculty of living in the present moment.

So the participants in a ritual have to be alert in the moment, and to place their attention not on themselves but on the task in hand. If there is nothing to be done, then nothing should be done. The mind should be kept free of pain and suffering. One way of doing this is to give the ordinary mind something to keep it busy. Mantras, prayers, observation all keep the mind busy and stop it from becoming self-involved.

What usually leads to self-involvement is the idea that one has been hurt either by commission or by omission. Imagined slights decrease self-esteem and injure one's picture of oneself. Sometimes we go as far as blaming others or, what is even worse, oneself, when we have suffered an accident or any other physical injury. All of these ideas distort our ability to receive the scents, sounds, tastes, touches, and images that fill each moment. By failing to register these impressions that are external to us, we become introverted and concerned solely with our own sense of importance or lack of it. This leads to a great loss of energy with the result that things get even worse and we become depressed and full of hate.

To avoid this, some lodges counsel members to strengthen the first moment of wakefulness in the morning. How we welcome a new day sets the tone to the rest of the day. So members are counseled that when they wake up in the morning, they should get straight out of bed. To lie in bed for that extra five minutes only encourages the mind to dream, or rehearse the day to come, and this dissipates the alerting energy that woke the system up.

To help conserve that energy, in one old system, the day starts with a greeting to Broda, the Lord of Necessity, who governs even the gods. Waking is a necessity and there are duties that belong to waking to be undertaken. Almost the first task of the day is, of course, to attend to the call of nature — and so we visit her altar in the smallest room. A good preparation for the rest of the day is to perform this activity swiftly and clearly, and then to wash. We arm ourselves with clothing, food, drink, and the tools of our trade, and we are ready to begin the day.

These activities, which are governed by necessity, are part of daily life. Even activities that may seem humdrum can be used as opportunities to wake up and acknowledge necessity. Whatever your personal morning routine is — you might be one of those who wakes up bright and sings loudly in the shower or one who drags his feet around for an hour — it is probably a mechanical rut that is performed with no consideration for anything other than yourself. This rut stops us from being receptive to all the impressions a new day brings. The greeting to Broda, the Lord of Necessity, at the start of the day shakes us out of a personal world by acknowledging something bigger than ourselves, and the alerting mechanism is thereby strengthened.

Each day has a beginning and an end. It is complete in itself. Within each day we start many new activities. To cultivate the sense of the present, each new activity should be approached afresh. In many systems, a meal is begun with a prayer so that the day, which is usually full of the hustle and bustle of activity, is punctuated with moments of recognition of something sacred which allows us to give proper attention to the new task. We are all aware of how, when we are totally absorbed in some problem, we walk around in some kind of daydream, mechanically going through the motions of the day, while our attention is absorbed with the problem. There are of course processes that take many days to complete, and this provides a sense of continuity to our activities, but we do not have to carry our past into the present as if it were a great burden. Each moment can be enlivened with new impressions. For this we need to recognize what is necessary at any given moment and act accordingly.

In days past, social customs emphasized the difference between days of work and the day of rest so that sacred and profane activities were kept distinct, and the ability to recognize the sacred and the profane was nurtured. However, as is inevitable, these rituals have lost their power to evoke the sacred within us and have degenerated into meaningless rules. So be it. In fact one could easily survey the present state of affairs and say that a considerable amount of time and energy is devoted to the deliberate breaking of the last two commandments in the Judeo-Christian Decalogue. "Thou shalt not bear false witness" (the press and media should take note). "Thou shalt not covet" whatever the advertising business recommends.

It is very easy to be negative about the present state of affairs. But that is futile, since it is the state we live in. What we *can* do is separate ourselves from that which is not real and keep ourselves clear of impurity. In order to strengthen that within us which is not concerned with lies and untruth, it is necessary to practice its presence, so that we become familiar with it and enable it to grow.

This growth does not come about through thought or imagination. If it did, we would all have wings and move at will through time and space. We would also be extremely dangerous — more so than any atomic bomb. Thankfully, what is within does not grow like that. Only by the regular acknowledgment of its presence can it grow. Each system has its methods — breath control, closely observed movements, mantras, yantras, prayers, prostrations, or consciously performed rituals. All these lead to the growth of that moral sense that recognizes the mechanical and the false. This moral sense does not censure or impose on others. This growth is the truth growing within you, so that you can no longer act against it. This takes time — probably a lifetime. But the process can be started at any moment, and doing it enables one to begin to separate the real from the false, the mechanically produced from the knowingly done.

A BABYLONIAN RITUAL

Well over three thousand years ago, in Babylonian times, the principles of cleansing the working space, both internal and external, were almost the same as today, and it is well worth quoting a ritual at length (adapted from S. H. Hooke, *Babylonian and Assyrian Religion* [Oxford: Blackwell, 1962], pp. 105ff.):

> In the month Nisan, on the fifth day, four hours before the end of the night, the High Priest shall rise and wash himself with water from the river; he shall go in before Bel, clothed in a linen garment. He shall make a prayer to Bel and Beltia: "My lord is the lord of Destinies. My lord is the Dragon Star who holds the ring and the scepter. My lord is the Star who possesses wisdom. My lord and my lady are the great stars."
>
> After this prayer, he shall open the doors, and all the other priests and singers shall carry out their duties. Two hours after sunrise, when the table of the two has

been set in order, he shall summon the exorcist who shall purify the temple. Then he shall sprinkle the temple with water from the great river. He shall sound the bronze drum in the midst of the temple. He shall bring the censer and the torch into the temple. When the purification is complete, he shall enter the chapel; then with the censer, the torch and the water font, he shall purify the temple and the chapel. He shall touch all the doors with cedar oil. In the center of the chapel he shall mingle incense and cypress, which he will heat on the censer. Then, after sacrificing a sheep, he shall purify the chapel and the carcass of the sheep shall be cast into the river. The High Priest is not to see the exorcism or him who sacrificed the sheep, neither shall he see the purification of the temple. After it is complete, he shall summon the craftsmen, who will bring out the golden heaven and they shall cover the chapel completely with it. Then they recite this invocation:

"They shall purify the temple
Marduk, dwelling in E-ud-ul,
Azag-sug, god who sprinkles with pure water,
Nin-a-ha-du, who hears the prayers;
Marduk will purify the temple,
Azag-sug will draw the design,
Nin-a-ha-du will set in motion the spell.
Begone, all evil that is within the temple!
May Bel destroy thee!
May you be cut off from where you are!"

Then all the craftsmen will leave.

The full ritual also requires the high Priest to be purified. All instruments should also be purified and, to quote again from the Babylonians, "You should purify the bronze drum with torch and with censer and with cleansing holy water." We shall quote again, at length, from this ritual later in the book when we deal with the making of the instruments. As you can see, there is a similarity between the Babylonian ritual and the one described earlier in this chapter.

The same principles can be applied at the start of constructing a building, for example. Before the foundation stone is laid, the ground can be purified in the same manner as in the earlier ritual. The placing of the guardians, if you remember, built imperceptible walls, and the floor and ceiling were also placed in position. So an actual building of bricks and mortar is not always necessary; what is required is physical space in which you can carve out the working area. A physical temple does make matters easier, since its presence stands as a constant reminder, but a space delineated by a circle of trees, stakes, or stones does as well, and it seems that this is how it was done in times long past. In principle, a temple or space is an instrument and as such should be dedicated to one main purpose. This limits the possibilities of its use, so other spaces or chapels are dedicated to and used for other purposes.

THE TEMPLE WITHIN

Ritual is an external form that enables inner change to take substantial shape. Now that we have delineated and purified our temple, how does it compare to the form within us? The basic principle is simple and can be easily derived. If someone is standing facing the sunrise, there is that which is in front and can be seen, there is that which is behind and is hidden from view, and there is that which is to the left and that which is to the right. There are also the heaven above and the place where one stands.

These external dimensions are mirrored within. The place where one is standing is figured on the outer surface of the brain. The heaven above is deep within. That which is to the left appears on the right side of the brain, and that which is to the right appears on the left side of the brain. That which lies in front is mirrored by sight, whose source is at the back of the brain. That which is hidden behind is the unknown, which lies before one. The temple within, as a whole, is figured in the medulla. Here there is a reversal from the rest of the brain, where the white matter is hidden by the grey matter: in the medulla the grey matter is hidden by the white of the nervous system.

The Lords and Ladies, the instruments, and the temple itself are conceptualizations of the mind within. They are symbols, allegories, and myths that make real to us the imperceptible, the unknown. We need to separate these elements in order to use reason and true emotion and then act. We externalize these mental conceptualizations in our ritual actions, thus enabling inner change to take place. If these things only remain as ideas in our minds, they remain unreal and have little effect; to substantiate them, we must act. It is said that everyone has a book in them, but of what use is that experience and knowledge? Unless that book is written or spoken, it does not affect others. Even the great teachers had to speak, to act, for their work to be of some benefit to mankind. If it was so with them, how much more so with us? Mankind grows by accumulating knowledge, understanding, and wisdom, but if it is not passed on, what benefit is there to others?

We started this chapter with a dinner party and it seems fitting to conclude with one. In the Christian Church, the altar is known as the Lord's table, and what is placed on it is for the guests, the congregation. The Christian communion service or Mass is an enactment of Christ's Last

Supper, which was a Passover meal. In Judaism, preparation for Passover involves a complete cleaning of the house. All traces of bread are removed from the house and only unleavened bread can be eaten during the week, that is to say, only bread made directly from grain, without any yeast or souring of the dough — bread, pure and simple. Passover is the purification of the year. It is a fresh start.

CHAPTER THREE

TIME AND TIDES

Purpose is the little light of faith that glows qui-etly behind the mind of the operator. Doubt is the killer of faith, the thief of purpose. Cast out doubt; give it no room in your house. Dispatch it, send it hence, let it go.

—Instructions to Members, Order of Sentinels

VISUALIZE A LARGE POOL WITH A CENTER STREAMING light in all directions. Around this center, circulating around the pool, are other centers, which are surrounded by other objects turning around them. You can see that the water in the pool is like a whirlpool surrounded by other smaller whirlpools. The light streaming from the center is going to be disturbed and broken up by the whirlpools around it.

We on the earth have spinning around us our moon. The earth and moon create two small whirlpools in space, and the influence of the other planets and their whirlpools affect us through the field of gravity; we are also within the great wind of light that streams constantly from the sun. Even that light ebbs and flows according to the tides within the sun. In our shadow, where we interrupt the light from the sun, the streams of particles alter the fabric of space. This is modified by our moon, which is sometimes in front of us, sometimes behind.

It is common to think of our planetary system as though it were a piece of clockwork. This is not so. Rather it is a sensitive creature with ebbs and flows. It almost seems to feed us: as our sun moves around the galaxy it passes through space, which has interstellar dust within it, and this dust is attracted to the solar system. It is the same with meteorite showers.

We live within this system, and its changes affect us. This is particularly obvious in the case of the moon. The moon affects all the liquid particles upon the earth, and where enough of them are gathered together in the oceans and the great lakes, its influence can be seen as tidal movements.

If you are on a ship in port, it makes sense to sail on a full tide, not only because you then have maximum water depth, but also because as the tide moves out, it carries you with it and this saves energy. To the seafarer, knowledge of the varying times of the tides is very important; we on land may think that tides do not affect us, but this is not so. We are over 90 percent water, and even though the changes might be slight and easily overridden by the will, the movement is taking place and, if caught at the right time, can add energy to our efforts.

ASTROLOGY

Astrology is an eclectic art. Although people have tried to turn it into a branch of science, these efforts do not carry much conviction. Its beginnings lie many millennia in the past, but oddly, after its formulation in approximately 450 B.C., the basic rules have remained more or less unchanged. Interpretations have changed with fashion. Chinese, Buddhist, and Indian astrologers, although they differ in their use of the system, agree to a very large degree about what the system means.

In astrology, the heavens are divided into twelve sectors from the standpoint of the earth. The sun appears to move through these sectors in the course of a year (of course, we know today that it is the earth that moves). The moon also appears to move, both through the sectors of the starry heavens and, on a daily basis, through the twelve corresponding divisions of the sky over the earth.

There are also wandering stars that change their position against the starry heavens; these are the planets of our solar system. "Planet" comes from a Greek word meaning "wanderer." Over the millennia they have acquired certain characteristics and have been assigned functions in the minds of astrologers. Astrologers have also assigned principles to the sectors or signs and areas of life to the divisions of the sky, which they call "houses." Because the planets wander through all the houses during the day, they are taken as adding to or taking away from the operation of these houses. As the planets wander through the signs, they are also reinforced, opposed, or left alone by the nature of the signs. The nature of particular planets also accords with particular signs.

The planets are: the sun, characterizing the nature of the being; the moon, characterizing how the nature is affected by its surroundings; Mercury, how the being communicates; Venus, the being's desires and habits; Mars, how its nature reacts to pressure; Jupiter, how its nature flourishes; and Saturn, how the being is self-limited. Of course, these meanings are oversimplifications, but they give a guide to how the planets can be used as symbols for activities.

The signs are familiar to everyone who reads the newspaper columns. They are Aries, the initiator; Taurus, the administrator; Gemini, the communicator; Cancer, the homemaker; Leo, the child and the teacher; Virgo, the harvester or the worker; Libra, the weigher of balance; Scorpio, the seeker; Sagittarius, the far-seer; Capricorn, the ambitious one; Aquarius, the unattached friend; and Pisces, the suffering servant.

The houses in order are: first, the house of doing; second, the house of possessions; third, the house of talk and travel; fourth, the house of the mother and natural magic; fifth, the house of lovers and children; sixth, the house of work; seventh, the house of partnership; eighth, the house of legacies, sex, and ancient magic; ninth, the house of far travel; tenth, the house of the father and the public; eleventh, the house of friends; twelfth, the house of hidden knowledge and esoteric magic.

It is clear from what has been said that astrology is a study in itself. For our purposes, however, because the planets rise and fall in the sky and their influences can be seen as rising and falling, astrology can be a convenient way of working out the best time to do things.

I CHING

In the East, the *I Ching* or *Book of Changes* is used. The theory of the *I Ching* rests on the supposed fact that the balance between two forces, the yin and the yang, is constantly in motion; when either of the two forces is too strong it automatically changes into its opposite. These forces are sampled either by casting three coins or by casting the stalks. Its operation involves the random dividing of a heap of sticks or stalks (or, alternatively, casting coins) and then counting them out so as to produce a figure called a hexagram — a structure of six lines, some of which are unbroken, some of which are broken, and some of which are change lines. While the casting is taking place, the thrower holds the question in mind, and for the space of that moment the coins and the thrower become one.

Because the question has passed through six stages, all aspects of the matter should have been covered.

There are two possibilities each time you throw, and if you throw six times, there are sixty-four possibilities in total ($2^6 = 64$), giving sixty-four possible hexagrams. The *I Ching* itself gives images and readings connected with each hexagram and with each line of the hexagram. If there is a changing line, a new hexagram is generated, with its own images and readings. The readings are based on the philosophy of change and are in the main open-ended, so that the readings in the text can be interpreted in the light of different questions and events. Someone can, for example, use it to consider whether or not it is a good time to undertake a task.

THE TAROT

The Tarot is a pack of cards in which the archetypes of thought and feeling have been clothed with imagery. It has overtones of myth, magic, ritual, and ceremony. The pack has two parts: the Major Arcana consist of twenty-one images, and a Fool or Wanderer which is numbered zero; the Minor Arcana consist of fifty-six cards in four suits, which correspond to the four elements. Each suit has fourteen cards, four of which are called court cards, because they represent Pages, Knights, Queens, and Kings. The remaining ten are numbered from one to ten and their significance is related both to their particular number and to the nature of the suit.

The logic of the Tarot is that in shuffling the pack the user becomes one with the event. As he shuffles, his inner state of being interacts through the unconscious with the way the cards are mixed. It could therefore be said that whatever order the cards come out in when they are dealt is a mixture of an outer event and an inner state, so the dealt cards can be used to interpret this interaction. If the operation is unconsciously confident then the order of dealing will show this. If a ritual is to be performed, the state of mind of the operator is all-important; methods such as the Tarot are a means of accessing this unconscious knowledge.

SYMBOLIC DIRECTIONS

Another method — a less familiar one — is that of symbolic directions. Each day comes under the rulership of a particular god. To list them in their traditional sequence (according to the ancient view of their relative distance from the earth): Saturn (Saturday), Jupiter (Thursday), Mars (Tuesday), sun (Sunday), Venus (Friday), Mercury (Wednesday), and moon (Monday). Each hour of the day also comes under these gods or powers. Each day begins with the planetary hour of its day. So, for example, Sunday from 12 midnight until 1 A.M. is ruled by the sun; 1 A.M. to 2 A.M. comes under Venus; 2 A.M. to 3 A.M. comes under Mercury; 3 A.M. to 4 A.M. comes under the moon; 4 A.M. to 5 A.M. comes under Saturn; 5 A.M. to 6 A.M. comes under Jupiter; 6 A.M. to 7 A.M. comes under Mars, and 7 A.M. to 8 A.M. comes under the sun again. If you keep up this sequence, you will find that midnight to 1 A.M. on the next day begins under the moon, and so on: each day of the week begins under its ruler.

If the operator of an intended ritual takes these symbolic hours into consideration, along with the astrological sign that the sun is in on that day, and the phase of the moon, then he or she will gain some guidelines about the state of affairs that prevails internally at the time.

Other methods include the symbology of the Kabbalistic Tree of Life, which is incorporated in the Galgal system.

A good account of this and other divinatory methods can be found in Cherry Gilchrist's book *Divination* (Dryad Press, 1987). Whatever method is used to deduce the correct time for setting up a ritual (a process called "election"), it is an attempt to perceive in some way the general state of the earth in the solar system and, in particular, the relationship of the temple's location to that system. Of course it would be very nice if one could perceive the unseen tides directly, but lacking such a cosmic view, we have to make do with what we have.

CONFIDENCE IN ACTION

When a person keeps a farm he pays particular attention to its size and its location — whether it is on flat or sloping ground, and how the prevailing winds strike it, whether it is good agricultural land or poor but useful for grazing, and whether it is to be used for arable crops, cattle, sheep, and so on. There are times when it is right to start plowing, planting and sowing, weeding, and harvesting. All the circumstances, including the nature of the community, need to be taken into account in order to come to the correct decision. So an entrepreneur, when setting up an enterprise, will also take everything into account that can affect the success or failure of the venture. Even a game of golf can be won or lost because of the weather or the players' confidence.

Anything that enables a person who is starting an enterprise to have confidence is important. It makes success more likely if you believe it is going to work properly. One could describe these matters as a form of self-hypnosis or a confidence trick, but that would miss the point. The human mind has its director, its will, and what damages the will is doubt. One should doubt the evidence, one should be aware that one does not know all the answers, but in every field of human endeavor it is absolutely clear that doubt kills the ability to carry things through to a successful conclusion.

Suppose, for example, that the room set aside for a ritual is to be used for the first time to confirm an officer of the lodge in his duty as a keeper of the door. The matter concerns limits — the authority to accept or send away. Such a person needs to display good judgment and to be willing to refer the unknown to higher authority. Properly constituted, a doorkeeper is a person under authority exercising the power of acceptance or rejection. The matter therefore comes under Mars.

As it is a question of coming to fruition, then the best time is when the moon is full, or at least well on the way to becoming full. It would be nice from all points of view if Mars could receive a good aspect from Saturn, the planet of authority; and it would be nice if Mars were in one of its own signs, Scorpio or Aries.

Supposing we can find a practically convenient time when these two conditions are fulfilled, we next have to find a time within that period when the moon is full or nearly full: this will narrow the period down to one or two days. Then, for these purposes, we would like Mars to be in the house of far-seeing, the ninth house; this factor will narrow the time down further to a few hours. We can now look at what the other planets are doing at the time, to fine-tune the timing, and to see how they will help or hinder the operation. The twelfth house of esoteric matters may be important; so may the magical planet Mercury. In practice, of course, one has to make compromises between favorable and unfavorable indications.

The time picked may be some distance ahead, but it is more important that it is conducive to the purpose. Having found a time that is reasonable for an important matter according to astrology, one should as a matter of course check with some other method of divination, such as the *I Ching*. If the conclusions and judgments of the two methods seem to reinforce one another, one can have some confidence in the date chosen: the two methods, one almost mechanical and statistical and the other apparently dependent on chance, agree with one another. It is now time for all those concerned to consider whether they also feel that this is a good time. If they honestly feel that it is, then the matter should be proceeded with. However, if those concerned feel in themselves that it is not the right time or that it is not the right thing to do, this feeling should take precedence over the results of the divinatory methods.

Although astrology has been stressed in the preceding example, if no competent astrologer is available, other methods can be used. Whatever primary method is used for picking a time, another method of divination should be used to check the results, and different people should be involved in this second method. It is a common fault that the same person is employed to use different systems of divination. Because the interaction of the operator with the method is the same, they are unlikely to make a different judgment. This is not an esoteric phenomenon: it is well-known in the field of accounting. If columns of figures one has added up do not balance, one goes through them again and tries to find the error. If you still cannot find the error, it is better to give the figures to someone else to check: having failed to pick them up a second time, the chances of your finding the error at all are vastly decreased. Your mind starts to see what it expects to see rather than what is actually there. Every editor knows this problem when proofreading for spelling errors.

Many people undertake the work of ritual in a sloppy and undisciplined manner, even though they may in their ordinary lives earn their living by being precise and disciplined as engineers, doctors, or bookkeepers. Artists in all fields know that success in their work depends on complete mastery of their tools and medium. The apparent abandon of the dancer is only achieved by much "blood, sweat, toil, and tears." How much more important, then, the necessary preliminary work is in those fields where rituals are to be carried out. In this respect, the clearing of the ground and the proper timing of things are vital to the success or failure of the task.

CHAPTER FOUR

RITUAL AND LANGUAGE

*Divinity speaks to each in their own tongue. What
then is the language of the Divine?*

—Instructions to Members, Order of Sentinels

WE DO NOT KNOW WHEN OR HOW HUMAN BEINGS
first began to speak. We could theorize that the first
spoken interchanges took place during courtship. Gestures
convey information, but they cannot be very precise.
Grunts, moans, squeaks, growls are still around today.
Crooning sounds can be heard when most mothers feed
their babies. Sighs of contentment and pleasure convey feelings and emotions. From the production of sounds to the
exact description of a language, rich in meaning, is quite a
leap — a leap to a symbolic form of communication.

In primitive tribes, the power of naming is considered
magical. In our European mythology, we love the fairy tale
of Rumpelstiltskin, whose threat could be overcome if his
name was known. In the Indian tradition, the power of
naming is the power to create. Even in the New Testament,
John begins his Gospel with "In the beginning was the
Word," while in the Old Testament, creation begins on the
first day with "And God said, Let there be light."

The oldest words that exist are sounded forward in the
mouth. "Mummy," "Daddy," "Ma," "Pa," "*Amah,*"
"*Abba,*" and their equivalents in other languages are usually the first words to be spoken by a baby. As children, we
are curious about the names of things and we are taught to
identify different things by learning their names. Naming

makes it possible for the attention to be fixed on particular things. Very young children often go through a phase of having an imaginary companion whom they name and talk to by name: it is as if the naming makes the companion real.

The "dictionaries" of olden times were the bards and storytellers, who knew the genealogies, legends, myths, and names of all things. Such knowledge was power; those with this power became the priests and rulers; "their word was law." After the ability to name, the next major development in language was probably when certain people gained the ability to portray animals, birds, and other things around them in such a way that they could be recognized by others. In time, these images became stylized and particular meanings accrued around them. Given the human ability to scan, where attention can be moved from left to right, right to left, up and down, or down and up, it was a short step to putting single, stylized images together to express a sequence of ideas. Information could now be conveyed in order. Logic had arrived in the external world. Ideas and concepts could now be exchanged.

In some parts of the world, these pictographs gave way to hieroglyphs, which could convey more complex ideas, because their images stood for a class of meaning rather than a single meaning. Hieroglyphs are symbolic rather than representational, and this allows for far greater economy. Whereas Chinese, for instance, which is a pictographic language, requires one to memorize up to five thousand separate images or pictograms, in Egyptian hieroglyphics a separate character eventually stood for a combination of a consonant and a vowel (such as Ba, Be, Bo, Bu, Bi).

The great breakthrough in the development of language was the invention of the alphabet where each sound was broken down and represented by single letters.

Contrary to received opinion, probably the oldest alphabet is in cuneiform script, which, with the advent of paper, could be written in ink rather than impressed on clay tablets. This had the immediate effect of reducing the bulk of records and making them more portable. The first use of the alphabet seems to have been the recording of straightforward commercial information.

Before the invention of writing, power resided in the memories of the elders and was only imparted to those who were felt to be worthy successors. The laws, the customs, and all the background knowledge had to be memorized and passed on. There were no maps, no histories that could be read independently. Once the written form appeared, information could be disseminated more widely. As long as scripts were pictographic or hieroglyphic, however, reading and writing were still limited to few people, and these scribes had great power. Only they were privy to carefully preserved rituals and other secret matters.

The invention of the alphabet completely changed the situation: the skills of reading and writing became accessible to the majority of people. The explosion of learning must have been comparable to that which appeared with the invention of the printing press. Anyone of moderate intelligence could be trained to recognize 22 to 30 symbols rather than the 60 to 150 of the syllabary or the thousands involved in pictography. Language had begun its demotic journey, which culminates in the present state of civilization, where even the most abstruse knowledge is available to anyone who can read and write. Of course, different languages exist, and one is limited by the languages one knows, but certainly an understanding of such languages as English and Russian affords access to enormous quantities of information.

A friend of mine was touring in Germany when his car broke down. No one in his family spoke German. They pushed the car to the nearest garage. They and the garage owner could not understand one another. My friend said, *"Können Sie Englisch sprechen?"* which was about the limit of his German. The garage owner looked up from the car and said, *"Nein, aber das Auto spricht Deutsch."* As a mechanic who understood the workings of a car, the car gave him its information in his own language: the car spoke German.

Where physical phenomena are concerned, languages can easily be translated. It is when the language reflects a psychological view that trouble arises. Each culture is based on a particular set of psychological views that is conditioned by climate, racial temperament, and religious and philosophical values. A language reflects these psychological perspectives, and to translate them from one language to another is problematic. George Bernard Shaw said that the Americans and the English are two nations separated by a common language.

Noam Chomsky, the world-famous researcher into the structure of language, argues that there is an underlying structure that is evidence of a deep-level operation in the brain laid down in the physical structure. This can cast some light on the higher feelings as well. Where religious experience is concerned, accounts of the experiences themselves in the various religious traditions differ only in minor detail. Yet there is often much argument between practitioners of the different religions. The *experience* of the transcendence of God runs through each religion. That God is love and is to be loved is a central focus of Islam and Christianity. Yet the religious beliefs and practices that express this common truth have developed differently in each tradition. If we look back at the historical relationship between Islam and Christianity, and the wars that have been fought between them, we may wonder if there ever was common ground. What differs between the Islamic and the Christian perspective is the *significance* each tradition has placed on the love and transcendence of God.

Once we start to interpret an experience, we rely on a particular psychological view, which is unlikely to be objective. This gives rise to battles. Those who share a perspective band together. If they are unable to accept the fact that other interpretations are also possible, then they fight with those who seem to take an opposing view. The reality of the experience itself is obscured and forgotten. It reminds one of the classic story of three people, each blindfolded, trying to describe an elephant. One describes the tail, another a leg, and the other the trunk. Their descriptions do not match, and none of them describes the whole elephant.

Ritual attempts to structure the psyche by bypassing the conscious or verbal mind so as to reach a certain order of psychological truth. In other words, it must bypass the level of interpretation and go straight to a level of experience that gives rise to shared meaning. The verbal mind, which is our interpreter, is limited by the laws of logical consequence. At this level, we have to make choices between this and that, a process that inevitably precludes alternate sets of possibilities. The choices we make also depend on conditioned values. In short, interpretation leads only to partial truth.

Ritual therefore must be powerful enough to enable the participants to experience that which is beyond their normal, conscious sphere. Even here problems arise. For example, what is the reality of noncorporeal beings, of inimical influences, angels, devils, spirits? There is no doubt that they have been experienced in some form or another by individuals of all cultures, but interpretations of their significance vary from culture to culture. Let us take the word *daemon*. The ancient Greeks used the word for an intermediate class of supernatural beings between gods and humans; they could be out there in the world, in some sense, but also each person had a *daemon*, which was the presiding force that steered one's life. In English, however, it has come to mean a demon, a malign force. In old Persia, the *daevas* were inimical, whereas in India their equivalents, the *devas*, are benign.

Any word undergoes a change of meaning in time according to the shared understanding of a particular culture. We can now no longer readily use the word "gay" in the old sense of being lighthearted. Yet we also retain in a sort of folk memory the old meanings of certain words or actions such as knocking on wood or throwing a pinch of salt over the left shoulder. In Wales, in my youth, girls would be asked by older ladies if their mother had a black-handled knife, which is a ritual knife used by witches. Masons shake hands in odd ways and exchange cryptic expressions such as "Is he on the square?" All of these are either relics of previous activities that have carried over into common usage or are rituals used to identify whether someone shares a common understanding.

Words also act as a bridge between what has been and what has yet to come. As new words enter a culture's common vocabulary they can act as indicators of possible future trends. We now talk of "single-parent families," "house-husbands" and "telecommuters." Will they become an inescapable part of our culture? What new psychological views will that give rise to? What will the teleculture demand of us? With such new words one can see how a common understanding is built up and shared.

Within a ritualistic context, the purpose of a catechism is to check whether you do share a common understanding and whether or not you are a real member of the congregation. In a ritual lodge, the doorkeeper plays the key role in identifying those who are entitled to enter. It is not a matter of personal recognition. The doorkeeper may know the people very well socially, but they must still be catechized about their knowledge before they are let in; conversely, it does not matter if they are strangers, because as long as they can answer correctly, with understanding, they are entitled to be there.

DEFENDING THE PSYCHE

But what about oneself? What about ideas and feelings coming from outside oneself? Are they likely to interfere with the integrity of one's psyche? Do you remember the childhood game of walking along the pavement without stepping on the lines between the paving stones? One often felt as though there were a real penalty to pay for stepping on a line, as though one would truly let the devil into one's life. Many children have these little rituals, which test their ability to cope with the bad influences of life.

What begins as play carries through into our adult lives, and we create various means of defending ourselves from bad influences. In primitive societies, people carried little talismans as protective devices, and even today many wear some form of symbolic protection. Charm bracelets are an example: the charms represent what people would like out of life. It is a form of sympathetic magic: the chosen symbols invoke good influences to protect them against bad luck. Necklaces are worn with various symbols as well; the stones in them are often birthstones. Traditionally crystals are used to magnify psychic influences. Christians wear the cross around their necks, in their lapels, even in their ears. Jews wear the Seal of Solomon, a miniature menorah, or tablets of the Law; Muslims the hand of Fatima or a phrase from the Koran. The list is endless.

In the game of life we are never sure what is going to happen to us, so we try to ensure that the balance of luck or chance will tip in our favor. We call on powers greater than ourselves and feel secure in their sphere of influence. We may live in a scientific and rationalistic culture, but why take chances? Perhaps wearing a moss agate ring will help. In Britain the continuing sales of the good-luck charm of the Cornish pisky known as Joan the Wad seem to imply that the uncertainty of life is well-recognized, and that any means to help tip the balance in one's favor will still be used. I have even known a famous chess player who would rather be late for a chess match than go without his St. Christopher medallion.

All these symbolic devices reinforce the human psyche's defensive characteristics and imply that there is a protective power. I suppose everyone has heard of the pentagram, which protects magicians against the terrible powers that they wield. This is yet another use of symbol: if you can confine the power in some way, you can control it. The story of Aladdin and his lamp deals with this; so does the story of the genie confined in the bottle under the Seal of Solomon. Magical alphabets, and magical symbols and names, were invented to call up these powers and confine them. Hence also the tradition of secrecy. If everyone knows what your world is composed of, then life is just as uncertain as it ever was. If someone knows your protective device, they may be able to counteract it. Secret symbols and protective devices are different means of helping to tip the balance of uncertainty in one's favor.

MAGICAL DEFENSES

A magical language is a psychological device created to direct the operation of the mind in specific directions. Like all languages, its basic component is an alphabet, and the ability to manipulate it depends on knowledge, skill, and experience. Consider the following alphabet:

Here is an alphabet of twenty-eight letters, consisting of three single elements, seven double elements, six triple elements, and twelve quadruple elements. If you examine it carefully you will see that there is a logic to its construction. Each element has an internal logic within the total framework, and if used like an alphabet, it would give you an underlying unifying structure to whatever was transposed into it.

$$\text{I} \mid - \mid \cup$$

$$\text{I}- \mid \text{I}\cup \mid -\text{I} \mid -\cup \mid \cup\text{I} \mid \cup- \mid \cup\cup$$

$$\text{I}-\cup \mid \text{I}\cup- \mid -\text{I}\cup \mid -\cup\text{I} \mid \cup\text{I}- \mid \cup-\text{I}$$

$$\text{I}-\cup\cup \mid \text{I}\cup-\cup \mid \text{I}\cup\cup- \mid -\text{I}\cup\cup \mid -\cup\text{I}\cup \mid -\cup\cup\text{I} \mid \cup\text{I}-\cup \mid \cup\text{I}\cup- \mid \cup-\text{I}\cup \mid \cup-\cup\text{I} \mid \cup\cup\text{I}- \mid \cup\cup-\text{I}$$

Most successful alphabets have a sense of wholeness and completeness about them; it is as if, quite apart from the meaning of the words, the actual written form conveys some other message. It is not only the literal sense, but also this aesthetic impression, that evokes the sense of wholeness. This is rather easier to see in Arabic or the Indian written languages than in English, except where the lettering

has been specifically designed by some great artist. Some alphabet systems, like Hebrew and ancient Greek, also assign numerical values to each letter, so that while reading you include not just a letter's shape and literal meaning, but also its numerical value, which gives rise to an even greater wealth of meaning.

Some magical alphabets use a grid system. For instance, if you draw up a five-by-five grid, and then place the English alphabet on it, leaving out the letter K (for which C can be used) or J (for which I can be used), you have a device for giving a new form to a word (see above).

Now take the name Broda. It will form a shape as illustrated at the top of the following page.

You could write out a complete passage in this manner and it would make no sense to anyone who lacked the key, the basic grid. If you knew of the matrix, however, your mind would strive to make some sort of sense out of the passage. In other words, the mind needs a trigger or a key to unlock that which is hidden. A magical alphabet is such a key, and by maintaining the tradition of secrecy it can be an effective defense mechanism.

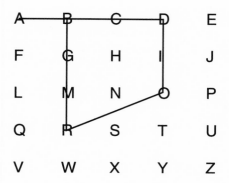

When the mind is presented with anything, it does try to make a whole out of it; this is the process of deriving meaning. That is why subliminal advertising is illegal — because it works. Even if a suggestion is subliminal, it will still trigger the mind into trying to make sense of the message, and may well influence our action without any conscious decision being made by the verbal level of the mind, which has been successfully bypassed.

In ritual many symbolic devices are used for defensive purposes, which may not make much logical sense but which our unconscious understands very well. You could say that symbols form the language of the unconscious. To be able to command the power of both the conscious and the unconscious mind is the true aim of the ritualist, but until that is a reality we have to use aids and supports along the way.

In the field of medicine, the fact of spontaneous remission of killer diseases such as cancer is well-known, but the reasons are not. We know that such imperceptible and nonlogical qualities such as will, faith, and belief are involved, but there is no guarantee that they will work in any particular case. People have been given up as hopeless cases by the doctors and have recovered. Others have been pronounced as cured, but the illness has suddenly returned in an even more virulent form. We do not know why. We can only foster those activities that include will, faith, and belief. The field of ritual includes such activities as the laying on of hands, the calling down of healing power, the remission of sin, and the removal of guilt. These are operations of will. But the proviso must always be, to use Christ's words, "Nevertheless, not my will, but thine be done."

Anything, therefore, that fortifies and strengthens will, faith, and belief must be seen in a positive light. If wearing a medallion blessed by someone in whom you trust helps you, why not wear it? If the performance of a weekly ritual strengthens your resolve, why not participate in it? It is so easy to say that all one needs is perfect faith and a strong will, but the means of acquiring them are often underplayed and forgotten. As in any other field, nothing comes without practice and attention.

Of course, the object of the work of ritual is to make one independent of such prosthetic devices; in the past and even now some people have been able to command the powers of their psyche without them. A group of people working together disposes of far more power than the sum of the individual powers. Ritual endeavors to organize such power to some definite end. We have referred in depth to the cleansing and preparatory work. In a lodge or a temple, the working space should not only be sealed but also defended against matters that may intrude in a negative way. To this end, magic circles are inscribed, amulets worn, medals carried, and instruments used which all have their particular functions. For example, it is almost a truism that a sword is used for defensive purposes. But it can also be used to direct attention. With a sword, you can carve tangible shapes and symbols out of the air. Such swords are very often inscribed with magical letters and have been psychologically imbued with particular powers. Within a lodge or temple each object used has been charged in a similar way for a definite end.

LIVING WITH LIFE

Recently the scientist Rupert Sheldrake has postulated a theory called morphic resonance. There are links between this theory and the notion of the Earth as a living being under the name of Gaia, which is a revival from the past when she was called Mother Earth. Morphic resonance is the esoteric doctrine of sympathy; that is to say, like affects like. The Gaia hypothesis postulates that the Earth, while possessing no great level of consciousness, still has the same imperative as all other living organisms, that is, to continue and survive in the most economical manner. It could be argued that the Green movement is part of the response of Gaia to the changes brought about by space flight. The earth is now surrounded by many satellites; these satellites, which were once part of its being (albeit an infinitesimal part), have now left the Earth, and it may well be that Gaia has a conservative reaction to this. One could say that humankind is at the threshold of a greater ecology and that Gaia is reluctant to accept the fact. It's a silly notion, of course, but maybe she doesn't want to grow up!

Conscious actions performed within that living being by the human race are bound to affect it through the principle of sympathy. To affect the mass of humanity is to affect the mass of life through the being of Gaia. In this context, it is interesting to note that one of the first worldwide television linkups seen in most countries of the world was the investiture of Prince Charles as the Prince of Wales.

Television screens all over the world were affected; people, animals, and atmospheres were affected. Neil Armstrong's walk on the moon was another such event. Great rituals affect the whole organism to a greater or lesser degree.

Ritual is myth, clothed in allegory, veiled in symbol. What is myth? Myth is a psychological truth. It is not a reasonable logical fact, but it enshrines a truth recognized by everyone in a particular culture. At the moment, in the Western world at least, the myth most people believe in is the scientific myth. This myth has its gods: the gods of time and space, the gods of causation. Within the parameters of its own belief system, it provides a reasonable explanation for all observable (and some nonobservable) phenomena of experience. It takes for granted the real existence of all those things it examines and accounts for everything, including intelligence itself, by means of some mechanism or other. Its heroes include Einstein, Newton, Boyle, Darwin, and Crick. In another age, today's physicists would have been called natural philosophers or metaphysicians.

The opinions of such people always carry as much or as little weight as their society allows them. In current society, the scientific worldview is regarded as real truth and as having all the answers (at least potentially). At the same time this worldview and its technology have enabled us to travel into space, where people have witnessed the awesome nature and size of our universe in a new way. These breakthroughs remind us to ask those questions that really matter and to which science does not provide the answers. What is humankind? What is its purpose? Is there good? Is there Divinity? These are psychological as opposed to logical questions. Crick and Watson's breakthrough in discovering the double helix of the DNA structure has given rise to the field of genetic engineering, and to a host of new moral questions.

There is a phenomenon called "Steam Engine Time." When it was the right time for the steam engine to be invented, then, quite independently, steam engines were invented all over Europe and North America. Perhaps the best-known example of this is the simultaneous discovery by Newton and Leibniz of the calculus of continuous movement, without which, we must suppose, there could have been no modern physics, chemistry, or engineering. It would have been a process of trial and error. The calculus could truly be called a magical alphabet, because through it the sciences were transformed. It changed our way of looking at the world and enabled us to give new form to our thought. Modern mathematics, physics, chemistry, and biology are truly symbolic languages. They have all the characteristics of a secret language: they are inaccessible to the ordinary person. The people who possess the keys to this language dispose of power. Nuclear weapons were made possible through this language, and whatever the rights or wrongs of their use, scientists do not as a rule stop working on something merely because it may become a tool of destruction.

Man is a curious being. As we discover new things, we unleash new possibilities that are capable of both destructive and constructive consequences. We do not know in which direction things will go, but is fear a good reason for us to curb our innate curiosity? Or should we learn to handle the power and responsibilities that new discoveries generate? Certainly fear arises. What tools do we possess to defend ourselves against these powers that we are afraid of?

Strangely enough, the antinuclear lobby has chosen a negative symbol, a symbol of destruction. It symbolizes a dead man, not a living man. What is needed is a symbol that channels and sums up the aspirations of mankind rather than its fears. Our aspirations set the direction of our lives and constantly guide our choices. Symbols speak for themselves and tell a story. It is curious to note that a number of countries have chosen the five-pointed star — the pentacle of operative and dangerous magic — as their symbol. Other nations have the six-pointed star, which is traditionally a symbol of balanced power. The six-pointed star is the "The Seal of Solomon the King," who was known as "the wise one." As a magical symbol it is used for purity and for establishing the correct relationship between that which is above and that which is below. The Maltese cross and the equal-armed cross are symbols of stability achieved through dynamic balance. They denote permanence and therefore a degree of inflexibility. A three-based symbol, however, such as the triangle, denotes instability whose constant movement concentrates a center. Perhaps the symbols nations use to represent themselves provide clues to their history and natures.

The Latin cross of Western Christianity is an archetypal sword or opened-out cube. The Islamic symbol has two aspects — the sickle moon and the hidden sun, represented by the crescent moon, which is beginning to reflect the light of the sun. Buddhism's symbol is a wheel with eight spokes, four spokes set against four. When one begins to understand the language of symbols there is a certain ironic enjoyment in appreciating the logos companies, sects, political parties, and so on choose, and how they tell us something about themselves. Symbols and symbolic languages speak to the level of the mind that deals with simplicity. They can be used to enhance or limit the operation of the human spirit. When we wear symbols, whether they are amulets or good-luck charms, we make a statement and declare ourselves to others.

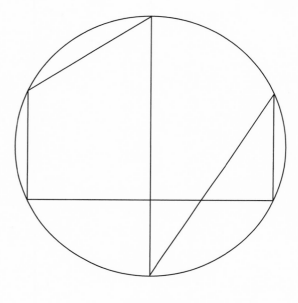

A puzzle

We will conclude this chapter with a little game. Draw a circle. Divide the circumference into six equal points (which is actually dividing the circle three times). How many different shapes can you make by joining the six points with one continuous line? You must not visit any point more than once, and you must finish at the same point you started from. One example is above. Do try it yourself first, before looking at the answers, which are at the back of the book!

CHAPTER FIVE

BOOTSTRAPPING

To make gold, you need first a little real gold.
—Instructions to Members, Order of Sentinels

THE MAIN PROBLEM FOR THE DEVELOPING NATIONS today is that they do not have the technology of the developed nations. They often have the resources — the raw materials and labor — but to utilize these, a developing nation has to start from the beginning by creating or borrowing technology and expertise from a developed nation. As payment for these goods and services, the developed nation requires a portion of the surplus produced. Unfortunately the developing nation needs that very surplus to provide itself with the necessary capital for further growth so that it can become technologically self-sufficient.

The only solution is for the nation to develop itself, to raise itself, as it were, by its own bootstraps. A similar problem besets the homeless. Because they have no home, they cannot cook, so they have to spend the money they get from begging on eating out, which is more expensive. So they can never save enough money to be able to pay rent and stop being homeless. Even if they do manage to save some money, the chances are that their appearance is so bad that no one will let them rent a room anyway. But once they have a room, they can wash, sleep, and cook. It is a starting point.

When you start on this work, you are in the same boat. As human beings, we have certain resources and energies, but because we live dissipated lives, we do not, at the beginning, have a sufficient amount of the right kind of energy to embark on this work. We waste our energies on useless thoughts, emotions, and actions. If you have a job, or are married with children, it is even worse, because so many different demands are being made on your energies and attention. It is a supreme juggling act. This problem is not new. The Christian parable of the wise and foolish virgins sums it up. The foolish virgins had spent their oil so that when the bridegroom came they had no oil to light their lamps, but the wise virgins had stored their oil and were ready for the bridegroom. To be able to collect and store the oil is a necessary first step.

A method has been evolved for beginning this work. This method is the making of magical weapons. It is used by many different systems, and each system might well have its own set of weapons, but the general principle remains the same. The set must be consistent and the weapons must be made by you, the user. Here, then, is the method for starting this work as used in the order with which I am most familiar. It requires a degree of commitment and dedication to complete the task, but it will be your work, your statement, and nobody else's.

THE KNIFE

Before you make a complete set of magical weapons, you first need to make a knife. It is important to make it from scratch and not just convert one you already have. First you need a whetstone — one of those stones used for sharpening sickles or scythes. It is usually about a foot long and fatter in the middle than at the ends. The next thing you need is some mild steel. It should be about nine inches long, an inch wide and about one-tenth of an inch thick. The rest of the materials you will require can be picked up in the countryside.

The next step is to make some thread. For this you will need to collect some wool from a sheep. In Britain at least you often see balls of wool caught in fences and hedges, so you can easily gather some. In fact any animal hair or fur will do. You should then comb out the wool. Lay it out into strips, each about three inches wide; place each successive strip so that they overlap each other. Roll the strips into a thin continuous sausage. As you feel the beginnings of a thread coming together, start twisting it so that it becomes a tight string. This doesn't take a great deal of effort, but it can be very fiddly. You are going to be using quite a lot of thread in making your instruments, so take time to get the technique of twisting it, and experiment to find out how much wool from the hedgerows you need to make how much thread.

While you are out looking for wool, you should also look for a stone with a sharp edge. The stone can be flint or obsidian or granite, or even hard slate. Use the stone to strip some bark off a willow, hazel, or ash tree. Then, still with the stone, cut the bark into strips about four inches long. In the meantime, you should also have made some glue by boiling down the skin and bones from a cartilaginous fish (such as a shark) or sheep's trotters or cow heel. The ensuing smells will, of course, make you very popular with your family and neighbors. Ah, well! There is no such thing as a free lunch.

When you are out looking for wool or a sharp-edged stone, while you are stripping the bark or indeed performing any action in the making of your weapons, it is vital that you keep your attention wide open. You should be aware of your *breathing*. All your senses should be alert and receptive. You should *hear* every single sound that there is to be heard, *smell* all the scents, savour the *tastes* in the mouth, *see* all there is to see, feel every *touch* on your body and skin — be aware of it all without going off into day-dreams or getting caught by any associations that may be triggered. Last but not least, every move you make requires an adjustment of *balance,* and you should try to catch each change as it occurs. Here are seven worlds, each different, each with their own information. These seven worlds combine in you; they interact within you to form your picture of the world.

Having gathered the materials — the glue, thread, bark, metal, whetstone, and an edged piece of stone — you can now start on the task of fashioning the knife. The piece of metal does not as yet have a point or edge and is difficult to hold, so the first thing we have to do is to make a handle for it out of the bark. The strips of bark should be dried gently in a draft of air and, when dry, soaked in the glue. The glue should be warm and tacky; one way of ensuring this is to put the pot of glue on some pebbles in a saucepan of hot water. *Cuisine ancienne!* You will have to keep the water simmering at a steady temperature. Using your fingers (not rubber gloves — they did not have them in the old days, though you could make a pair of tweezers out of bent twig), take a strip of well-soaked bark and lay it on the part of the metal that is to become your handle. Pad it out well with as much bark as you need, until you have built up a good, graspable handle. Then let the whole thing dry out.

Your attitude while doing this task should be completely attentive to the job in hand. If you find that you are daydreaming or thinking about something else, STOP. Draw your attention back to the task and start again. One way of doing this is to open up your senses. Smell the glue, feel it, be aware of the taste in your mouth, hear the sounds, watch the tensions in your body, and keep in touch with your breathing. One of the things you will learn is that your reaction to the smell of the glue is learned and conditioned. The

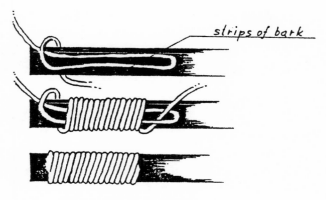

Whipping the knife handle

smell itself is neither nice or nasty: that is simply your judgment on it.

Before the glue is completely dry and it is still just the slightest bit sticky, take the thread that you have made and lay it along the handle. At the blade end of the handle, turn the thread back to the other end. You now have a double length of thread laid along the handle; tie a slipknot around the first end of the thread, leaving a loop for later. Then start laying and winding the thread around the handle all the way along its length. This is called *whipping*. When you reach the end nearest the blade, slip the thread through the original loop, which should still be exposed. Now pull the first end tightly and it should pull the thread underneath itself. Next pull both ends taut and cut the extra bits off with the stone.

The usual working conditions apply throughout this operation. If your attention wanders off at any time, STOP WORK! Recollect yourself by opening the senses and start again. This will happen many times.

It is now becoming obvious that you will need time to make the weapons. If you lead a busy life, then you have to make time. Set aside an hour a day and insist that you be left alone. It will be difficult at first, but after a while the rest of the household will leave you alone. You do not have to shout at them; your attitude must be matter-of-fact — "Well, this is how it is." Neither should you try to explain what you are doing; just say that you are working. It is no use trying to explain unless the other person is going to do the same. If there are other people doing the same work, do not work together. This is your work and nobody can help you. Don't use any modern aids either. This is "bootstrap" work and you have to start from the very beginning.

When your knife handle has dried out, you will need to dye it. Make a dye with oak apples — the little round balls you find on oak branches. Break them open and leave them to soak in water for a long time. Eventually you will get a black liquid with which you can dye the handle. You now have the beginnings of a black-handled knife.

The next task is to grind down a cutting edge to the metal. This part of the job is long, repetitious, and very boring. Now the way you have learned to work begins to pay dividends. You will find that as you grind away the edge on the whetstone, your attention will slip away quite often. Don't get angry with yourself. Don't lose heart. Just stop, bring your attention back to the task, and start again. You will find that you go into automatic, your actions become mechanical, and your attention keeps wandering. Simply stop and start again. At first you will find that you can't keep it up for much more than twenty minutes. Take a break for five minutes and start again. In any case, do not go over the hour you have allotted yourself to do this work. The whole process of grinding down the metal is going to be long and arduous, so pace yourself well. You will also have to shape the blade and its edge so as to give the knife a long point. The grinding is best done under running water; it would, of course, be very nice if it could be done in a stream, but a tap may have to suffice.

The next job is to obtain a large sandstone block. It should be roughly twice as long as it is wide and square in section — say, 2'6" x 2'6" x 5'. Don't try to smooth it off yet, as it is to be used as your working surface! You could use granite, but granite is harder to work with and probably too expensive for most people.

Now you should make a drill — an ancient device for boring holes or starting fires. For this you require a small block of hardwood, something that will sit comfortably in the palm of your hand, and in the middle of it you should carve out a small depression. You also need a piece of springy wood that can be bent into the shape of a bow as well as some thread — more searching of the hedgerows! Cut a notch at each end of the springy wood — with your black-handled knife, of course — and tie the thread across the notches until you have a basic bow. Take a piece of hazelwood, about nine inches long and as thick as your middle finger, and loop it round the string of the bow. The ends of the hazelwood should be slightly pointed. Place one end into the small depression in your piece of hardwood, which is held in the hand above the string of the bow. Place the other end of the hazelwood on your working base. When you move the bowstring backwards and forwards, the drill will turn in its hardwood bearing. If you want to make a fire, you should pile small shavings of soft wood (such as pine) into a borehole in your working base. If you wish to make holes with the drill, slightly wet the end of your hazelwood and dip it in some sand before drilling.

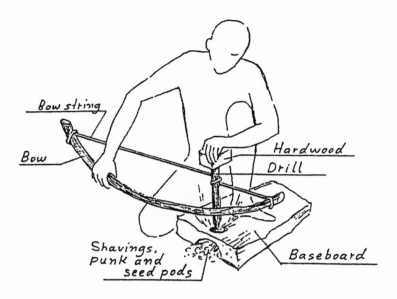

The drill

With a great deal of patience and careful attention you can bore holes even in metal using this method. Remember, the usual working rules apply throughout all this.

THE SWORD

Using your black-handled knife, you should next make a much longer knife (at least twelve inches long) to serve as a sword. It should be long enough for you to feel as though you are carving the air generously when you wield it. The blade should also be broader, say, one-and-a-half inches wide. Having decided on the exact proportions for the blade, you will need to acquire some more mild steel. The sword is made on the same basic principles as the knife, but it needs a handle with a guard to stop the hand slipping down the blade.

The design of the handle and guard should be kept simple, since they will be carved with the knife. The handle should be made out of a white wood such as poplar, ash, or willow. Choose your wood and then, with your knife, carve out two pieces at least four inches long until they fit your blade exactly. You will then need to bore some holes so that you can fix the handle to the blade. You can use the long point of your knife to bore out the holes in the wood, but to make holes in the metal you will have to use the drill and coarse, sharp sand. This again requires a great deal of care and patience, but do remember the instructions in the above section. You should eventually have six holes, two in each half of the handle and two in the metal. You will need to fix

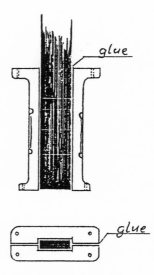

The sword handle

the handle temporarily to the sword while you go through the process of giving the blade an edge. If you tie some thread through the holes, the hilt should be secure enough for you to hold while grinding. Once you have got a clean edge, discard your temporary threads.

Before you can fix the handle on permanently, you will have to bore four more holes in the guard of your handle, so that later you can intertwine thread through them. Then back to your stove and to the delectable task of cooking more fishy glue. Stick the two pieces of wood onto the metal blade. Make sure the glue does not block up the holes in the metal, since you will shortly be threading wool back and forth through the handle and these holes. Once the glue has dried, strengthen the handle further by lacing white, undyed wool through all the holes appropriately.

THE CUP

Next comes the making of the cup or bowl. This can be done in your local pottery class. But do ensure that you work at it in the proper manner. One's mind tends to wander enough on its own even without all the distractions from the other people in the class. Ideally you should fire the clay yourself in a kiln of your own making, but as fire is a purifying agent anyway, I see no objection, in principle, to firing the bowl in the evening-class kiln. Don't glaze the pot, but you may decorate it with wavy lines (to symbolize water). When it has been fired, check it for cracks. If it is cracked, you will have to make another one. If you cannot get any clay, you could make a bowl out of sandstone, by grinding a bowl-shaped depression in the sandstone. Or you could carve a bowl out of a block of wood using your black-handled knife. By the way, if you use any tools for shaping the pottery bowl, make sure they are made by you with your knife and drill.

THE WAND

The wand should be about two and a half feet long — whatever is a comfortable length for you — so that you are able to hold it above your head and direct and point with it. It should be made of two different types of wood. One length should be a hardwood such as apple heart or black-thorn. The other piece should be a soft, white wood such as hazel, ash, or willow. You may wish to shave your woods with your black-handled knife to get a smooth surface. The two lengths of wood should, of course, be of a similar thickness and length, as you will need to join them. To do this, make a slanted cut, about four to six inches long, at one end of each of your two pieces of wood. Put the two slanted ends together so that they overlap, and bind them together with some very fine, strong thread (which you will have to make yourself) and whip along the length of the slant. Wet the thread before you whip it so that, as it dries out, the thread will shrink tightly onto the wood. Drying it out in strong sunlight will help.

THE CLOTH

Now to the making of the cloth. It may be difficult to obtain enough raw wool from the hedgerows, so your best bet is probably to get unwashed wool from the appropriate suppliers. You could buy a loom and learn to weave while you are about it, but this can be quite expensive. Once you have unwashed wool, it is quite easy to weave some cloth

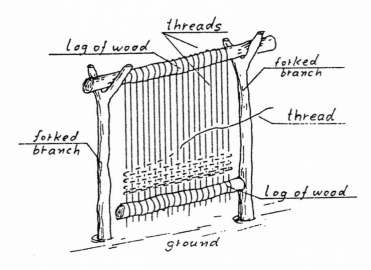

The cloth

by going back to rudiments. More wood and a little
patience is all that is required!

Find two pieces of forked wood and two more sticks of
equal length. The height of the forked branches will establish the length of your cloth, which should be big enough to
cover your knife, sword, bowl, wand, and stone. You will
need strong forked pieces of wood several inches longer
than the length of the cloth. Hammer the two forked pieces
of wood into the ground until they are secure posts. Cut
threads of the wool to the right length and tie each end to
your sticks: one of these sticks rests between the two forked
pieces of wood, the other stick weighs the threads down, as
in the illustration. You can now simply weave some wool
through your threads. You could also make smaller strips of
cloth and then sew them up, which would give a patchwork
effect. Remember that the usual working conditions apply.

THE STONE

You already have a large sandstone block, which you have been using as your working surface for all the other tasks. All that remains to be done is to make the top surface smooth. If you want perfection, you might wish to square and smooth the sides and base as well, but this is not really necessary. To smooth the surface you will need to get another, smaller piece of the same type of stone. Rub the two stones together, adding a little wet sand in between them. You will generate heat and the sand will dry out. Keep wetting it. This is another long and repetitive job for which the usual rules for work apply. So keep alert!

MAKING IN GENERAL

As you work, you may find at the back of your mind a certain feeling about the work. It may be a seed of sureness. If you have kept at it up to this stage, there is obviously something in you that has kept you going. If you can become aware of this "something," try to keep it in mind as you work. If you lose the sense of it, go back to it time and again. This will strengthen it.

Throughout the making of the magical weapons, the instruction has been not to use any modern aids, but to go back to basics. This is not because you are on some survival course, but you are returning to basic human endeavor. Stories about castaways — *Robinson Crusoe* and all its countless imitations, old and new — highlight basic human endeavor. Lost, isolated, and deprived of all that they had taken for granted, these castaways are thrown back on themselves and by their own efforts have to build something new. These myths serve to remind us of our past and our beginnings.

In Britain we have no records prior to the Romans because we did not write on stone. We were probably a wood culture, with wooden buildings and wooden tools. In fact, there still survives a word in Welsh that means "the writing on wood." If a wood culture really existed, then a damp climate such as ours would quite quickly destroy all traces of it. Tradition often keeps alive some information about the past, but these islands have been invaded often, and as each wave of invaders brought with them their own traditions and myths, it is now impossible to sort out what belongs where. This has also caused us to forget the ways in which things used to be done. Even in recent times two World Wars have broken the old molds and we are now in transition, forging new ones. What will survive, what will be accepted in a hundred years' time, we have no way of knowing. Many things will be different.

But whatever reminds us of our beginnings recapitulates in a very real sense the process from primitivism to tribalism to nationhood. This process can be thought of as occurring in each person's lifetime. A baby is fairly primitive in itself; its needs are simple and direct. If a baby cries for food, no amount of cajoling is going to stop it; it demands immediate response. Babies are totally dependent on others for their survival.

As children grow, they become more independent and learn to curb their instinctive demands. Through their games, their parents, and their teachers they begin to acquire the tools that allow them to gain some control of their world. Thus the primitive, warring factions within them soon begin to form tribes. Behavioral patterns emerge. These inner tribes fight for supremacy during adolescence, and whichever tribe or set of behavioral patterns wins sets the dominant note for that person's personality. As we mature, we begin to accept, perhaps a little more graciously, the existence of our different parts, so that there are fewer wars within us. A new unity comes into being such that each individual can become his own nation and wisely govern the various parts of his nature.

If you have completed the making of these magical weapons, what you have done, in the first place, is acquire some tools with which to make further tools. In making and wielding the sword, you will have gained some sense of carving out the air. You will have begun to appreciate what that element is. With the wand, you will have gained experience of the direction of energy. In making the bowl, the feeling of containment, the holding of liquid, will have been brought home to you; and when you finish off the surface of the stone, the nature of materiality will become real. In making the thread and the cloth, the ability to weave together will have been understood. You will also have learned patience and the ability to hold your direction; you will have strengthened your own nature and you may well have an appreciation of what your motivation is.

TEMPERING THE KNIFE AND THE SWORD

You have yet to temper the blades of your knife and your sword. Start a fire. You may use flint and steel, but preferably use the bow: it's not difficult. Once you have got the fire going, fan it to a red heat. Wrap the handle of your knife in a wet rag and put the blade into the fire. Have a bowl of water handy and when the tip of the knife is a bright cherry red, take it out and dip the point into the water. Watch the tip carefully. You will see a rainbow of colors running up the blade from the point. Dip the whole blade into the water and see what color has been fixed on the blade at the point. Repeat the process. When you feel confident that you can see the colors, then when blue appears on the tip, plunge the whole blade into the water very quickly. You have tempered your blade. It should now cut better when you resharpen it. By the way, do keep the handle covered with a wet rag; otherwise you will destroy the handle, quite apart from burning your hands!

You should also temper the sword in the same way. After you have finished sharpening the edge, remove the temporary threads from the handle and cover the exposed metal with a thick, wet rag before beginning the tempering process.

THE CORD

You now need to make a cord. This should be long enough to go easily around your waist three times. The cord should be made of three triple strands of thread — nine strands in all. You should wet the strands, twist them tightly together and leave them to dry with a weight on them. Once dry, the three triple threads should be wetted and twisted together again and left to dry out. You will then need to whip the ends together using the same technique you used for the wand. Now you have the tool for binding the elements together in due proportion.

THE CREATIVE

So far, we have *made* tools. This is a function of the creative within. It does not matter that the tools are crude and not very effective. They may look clumsy, but that is not the point of the work. It is the doing of the work that is important, the actual effort involved and the bringing of that effort to a conclusion. Some people are better with their hands than others, but one of the descriptions of this work is "the temple not made with hands."

The Creative exists in all beings, and it is our task, as conscious human beings, to gain access to that creativity so that it is expressed through us. Imaginary activity that takes no form does not affect creation in the slightest. We must empower our ideas with our imagination and bring them to fruition. The unwritten poem or book, the imagined picture, are incomplete creations without material reality. One of the tenets of the traditional approach is that everything must be "brought down to earth."

There is creativity in each of us, which is a reflection of the Creative. It is not the Creative as it is in itself, but as it is in us. It is easy for us to see the creative in us, and assume that it is the Creative itself. In other words, we assume that what we perceive is all there is. Rather than understanding that it is only a particular viewpoint, we extend our particular view and impose it on others as well. Not only do we mistake the creative in us as the Creative, but we also assume that it is the same in other people, that it takes the same form and has the same results in them. We are therefore guilty of creating a barrier between the Creative and the world rather than letting the Creative reflect through us into the world. If you think of your boss or your teacher or your president or your monarch as being the greatest, you leave no room in your world for a greater, and you are bound solely to your own view.

What we are doing in this work is trying to make a link between the creative in us and the Creative itself. This link may well be tenuous and slight, but it is a means of allowing something greater to enter our world. It is a means of being in command of ourselves rather than subject to another's view of the creative in themselves. That is why one makes the tools for oneself and on one's own. We only have to look up to the heavens and the vast expanse of space to realize that the Creative takes many forms, in many beings. One must respect this. If you know that others have done what you have done and if you know the effort it has involved, you begin to respect the work of their hands.

A final note: Traditionally, the black-handled knife was used to cut the umbilical cord and so to sever the final physical ties that bound the child to its mother. If we, as human beings, had not cut our umbilical cord, we would never have started the journey that resulted in a man standing on the moon's surface. We would never have seen the sight of the cloud-shrouded blue of the earth from space. We, as a species, will no doubt stand on other planets, in other solar systems, in the future. We have started on a long journey. We have lifted ourselves by our own bootstraps.

CHAPTER SIX

THE TRAINING OF AN APPRENTICE

*The apprentice says, "Very good"; the journeyman
says, "Good"; but the master says, "Not bad. . ."*
—Instructions to Members, Order of Sentinels

APPRENTICESHIP

IN ORDINARY LIFE, EMPLOYERS TAKE IT FOR GRANTED
that a student fresh from school or university is not much
use in the organization — at least not at the beginning. He
may be full of promise, but the ability to turn theoretical
knowledge and potential talent into practical application
requires time and opportunity. A good manager and
employer turns, with a firm hand and an eye to the future,
to the task of providing the right conditions for the new
and untried employee to flourish.

In the past, the way the employer did this was straightforward enough: the person was apprenticed to a master of
a trade, usually for seven years. Very often parents had to
pay some money to the master, and the apprentice lived
with the master's family as a sort of servant. In those days
the master usually lived at his or her place of work. At first,
all the apprentice did was to fetch and carry, clean and perform all the menial tasks of the enterprise. If many apprentices were employed, the new apprentice would be at the
beck and call of the others as well.

Close to the beginning of his apprenticeship, the new
apprentice would be captured by the others and put
through some terrifying ordeal. This usually had a genital

element and the apprentice would be blindfolded and/or naked. He would be interrogated at great length, and the others present would mock and deride him. When this little ritual was over and the new apprentice had passed the test, he would then formally be accepted as an "entered" apprentice. If any of them failed and ran away, the master, who had taken over the parents' role, had the right to call upon the law to apprehend and punish the runaway.

Those who have served in the armed forces or have been to one of the more traditional schools may recognize this process. In St. Andrew's University in Scotland, first-year students are adopted by older students who become their "mothers" and "fathers" and are presented with gifts — traditionally a pound of raisins. The "parents" then put them through their paces. At the end of a rather drunken and chaotic day the new students are accepted and become part of the extended family, and there is a shared sense of responsibility that lasts for their entire period at university.

Of course, these types of rituals lay themselves open to abuse of power, to cruelty and bullying. It could be argued that this overt process of challenge is particularly masculine in its method. For women, the process is more subtle in our modern society. In primitive societies, the methods of initi-ation into womanhood existed, but we do not apparently use them very much these days. However, they are there. When my wife and I had lived in our street for three years, we still knew nobody apart from our next-door neighbor. My wife became pregnant and as soon as the pregnancy was obvious, all the ladies in the street were introducing themselves to her, inviting her over for coffee; when her child was born, large bags of clothes suddenly appeared. This underground organization had gone on under my nose all the time, but I had not seen it. Only a woman knows the reality of "joining the club," the ticket to which is carrying the first child.

To join in any clique takes time unless, as in the above example, it is part of the natural process of growth and development. Rituals of entry into a clique of any kind help to ease the entrant in. These rituals usually take the form of some ordeal because such situations momentarily break down conditioned patterns of response so that the spirit of the entrant may be glimpsed. This works both ways: the entrant glimpses the spirit of the clique as well.

Time is also needed to understand the others involved, to get to know all the details that go to make up that particular group or club or band, so that it is possible to work together. This is certainly necessary if a group chooses to work democratically. Groups in which there is a strong hierarchical structure need only loyalty. The leader gives the order, and others obey all the way down the line. This hierarchical structure seems to be preferred by men, who are often not very democratic in the way they operate. Loyalty is given and received and men can act from that basis. Women are less capable of taking orders from a leader and acting irrespective of their personal feelings. They have to be totally comfortable with the situation, which is why women spend hours arguing and turning over possibilities and motives. Men often have little patience with this. However, if all the women concerned reach agreement, the matter goes ahead so swiftly that it is as if there had never been any doubt about it at all!

There are rituals surrounding the way decisions are arrived at. In the case of a strict hierarchical structure, the council to the leader gives advice, but it is the leader who decides. If a person objects, he must resign or be fired by the leader. This can lead to phenomena such as fascism and state communism. Even in democratic societies, however, which may have some means of representative government incorporating the principle of consensus, it is ultimately only a few who are the decisionmakers.

The alternative situation calls for decisionmaking procedures based on feeling. Here a matter is seemingly inconsequentially brought up, people chatter about it, the feeling is sounded out and this goes on until a general feeling is established. The matter is then resolved without any formal decision being made, but everyone present feels that the resolution is binding. Many decisions in families are made in this way; it is so familiar that it is easily overlooked by more formal organizations as a concrete method of decisionmaking. In Britain a great deal of small business is transacted at the pub, or while waiting for the children at the playgroup, or while having coffee or tea with the neighbors.

In the field of ritual it takes time to join the working group and to understand how it works. A lot of hard work is necessary to develop the abilities and skills of an apprentice ritualist. Can you work with others on the level of correct and immediate response? Do you have to be told what to do? Do you have to learn by heart? Do you need to know the reasons before you can do anything? Do you learn best by doing? Can you control your own immediate responses and subordinate them to the job itself? Can you keep your mind on the task for the length of time required? Are you reliable even if you are ill? In the field of ritual, all these questions have to be answered in the right way.

PROFESSION

In the field of mechanical engineering, an apprentice has to produce, in a given time, what is called his "test piece." This is usually an extremely difficult piece of work requiring precision and must be produced under pressure. The exactitude of such work is measured in seconds of arc and thousandths of an inch. It has to be as perfect as possible in the given time. The work has to be done regardless of his state of mind, whether he is ill or healthy, whether his heart is in it or not. To put the matter in context, a heart surgeon is not expected to let his private life interfere with his skills. We take this kind of behavior for granted among professionals.

Whereas surgeons and doctors come under the discipline of medicine (with all its rituals, in the operating room, for example, to ensure the correct interaction between the various members of the team and the optimum conditions for the surgeon to carry out the task), the general task under which a ritualist comes is the enhancement of the human spirit. To become an apprentice in ritual one needs to have completed one's "test piece" — that is, to have made the magical weapons.

The apprentice then has to start gathering information and becoming completely familiar with the chosen branch of ritual. If it is to be ritual healing, for instance, then the apprentice must learn about all the herbs and plants that are available, how to administer them, when to use them and when not to, and in what proportion, and how to prepare them as salves, pills, liquids, oils, teas, etc. He or she has to understand the doctrine of signatures whereby the plant itself, through its particular shape or markings, declares its possible uses. Or again, if the chosen branch of ritual is to be in the field of divination, then all systems of divination must be researched and their symbolic language and significances appreciated. The apprentice also has to learn the methods by which the operator of any system becomes the diviner. In astrology, learning the mechanics of the system can take three years, but mastering it at least seven. The same can be said about other systems: to learn the rules thoroughly is one thing, but to be an artist in their use is another. Artistry can only be achieved through constant practice. So by mastering the system's rules and regulations the operator can become the diviner or the healer.

In the period of apprenticeship one is usually under individual supervision while one learns endless rules, which may or may not be explained. Some people are simply told what they have to do. With time and cumulative experience they will acquire a measure of judgment and the reasons for particular actions will become apparent. This knowledge too is part of what it is to be a professional.

PROBLEMS OF PARTNERSHIP

A was apprenticed to Ritual Master B and she completed the task of making all the instruments in three years. B sent her off to a northern town where there was a job going as a maid in the house of a rich family. A did not like this at all — she was a graduate in English — but she wanted to continue to develop her abilities. Just as she was getting used to her new situation, she was told to return to the town where B lived. This involved a lot of upheaval, including explanations to her newly acquired boyfriend who knew nothing of her interests in ritual work.

Only much later did she realize what was going on. She thought she had been sent to the house because of the discipline of serving as a maid. In fact it was because of the housekeeper, who was an adept at reading the cards and tea leaves. But A had judged the housekeeper, who had a very broad Scots accent, a silly and ignorant woman.

Not long after she had finally settled down in the same town as her ritual master, she was looking forward to a lazy, sunny holiday on a beach with her boyfriend. Instead she was told to take a cycling holiday in Brittany. Her long-suffering friend objected, with the result that she was faced with the difficult choice of either explaining all her unpredictable actions or having him walk out on her.

This is one of the most awkward areas in ritual work. Close relationships are affected in one way or another by this kind of work. Even relationships between people who share these interests can be problematic, because this work *does* change one. It does not change one's core (except to make that core stronger), but it does change one's behavior, and when two people are changing, usually at different rates, then the other has to adjust to the change. Each of us, however, has preconceptions about what our partner is like, what he or she is capable of, and even what his or her motives are. Often our preconceptions create a prison for the other person. For the couple to have a creative relationship capable of surviving through growth and change, each has to know and trust the other. There also has to be no element of competition between them, and one has to trust oneself.

There is no reason that a relationship between two people, only one of whom is interested in ritual work, should not be successful. But it has to be based on trust and a clear recognition of the difference of interests, so that each can, without undue jealousy or curiosity, leave the other to pursue his or her own direction. As has been said before, no one can help you with this work; it is something that you must face on your own, so that such a relationship can positively help in your development as a ritualist.

In the event, A told her boyfriend that she was receiving instructions in religious matters and if he wanted her, he would have to put up with this sort of thing happening. She loved him, but she also loved the Divine, so there was no real contest. The boyfriend agreed not to interfere in her religious training. Things don't always work out like that. As each situation is different, an appropriate solution has to be found that deals with each problem on its own terms.

During the apprenticeship, the ritual master will give tasks to apprentices that will stretch them physically, emotionally, and mentally and will enable them to discover their capabilities. Apart from the enormous amount of information that has to be memorized and digested, the master will press apprentices into work they regard as beneath their dignity or beyond their capabilities. It is a time for the apprentices to realize their own strengths and weaknesses, and to establish how committed they are to the discipline.

The process of discovering our strengths and weaknesses is important to a human being, because we are generalists. As Mark Twain said, "What one fool can do, so can another." Other species are better equipped than we in terms of senses and abilities. We do not have our abilities given to us by nature. Where the human species wins out over other species is in its ability to organize its senses in new ways and its ability to structure new tasks.

THE JOURNEYMAN

The skills acquired during apprenticeship should enable one to make a moderate living. *Moderate* is the operative word, since the kind of energy and commitment required to be a successful professional in the world detracts considerably from this sort of work. In theory, one should be able to combine a successful career with mastery in the field of ritual, but in practice it is difficult to ride two horses at the same time. Any ambitious person could tell you how sacrifices are constantly made for one's career; families, moral values, time, and energy are all sacrificed on the altar of success and fame. Everything is geared and channeled to one end. Unless you are born into a position of material independence, you will have to sacrifice significant achievement in the world in order to undertake the work of a ritualist.

At the end of the apprenticeship, the master usually kicks the apprentice out. This used to happen quite literally. It was the ritual severance of dependence on the master and the beginning of journeyman status. In the old days, journeymen would then travel to different regions, taking on jobs wherever they went. Their test pieces would be their passport. They knew the rituals of greeting and signs for recognition, so they were accepted into new jobs. In the Sufi tradition, the Sufi would be passed from a master in one trade to a master in another, until eventually they knew something of many trades. By becoming jacks of all trades they continued to learn new skills.

You reach journeyman status when you begin to have some real idea of what it is you are doing. As a ritualist you would be a useful addition to any lodge. You should be capable of instructing the new apprentices in the various relevant branches of knowledge and skill. The motto of the journeyman is "learn and teach." The journeyman must be able to stand back from his own training and reformulate what was done to him so as to pass it on to an apprentice.

Journeymen are no longer dependent on a particular master. They are on their own, and it is their own responsibility to advance further in their chosen work. If they are sensible, they maintain a connection with their old masters and fellow journeymen. But now they have to contribute, in some measure, to the common good.

What does a journeyman ritualist have to do? As an apprentice, he or she will have learned how to hold an image in his mind for an hour at a time. He will have learned how to maintain direction in the midst of life's distractions. He will have learned to keep contact with what is real within him, even in the throes of passion. He will have learned something of the uneven tides that move the hearts of men. He will be independent of the movements of fashionable views and capable of taking a long-term view of humankind's apparent tragedies. This will make him a more conscious member of the human race.

Now he will have to put into practice what he has learned. Once he has been kicked out, the journeyman must quickly pick himself up, move on and start practicing his trade. There is no more time for indulging in preparatory work. A very common cry at this stage seems to be "I must gather more information and really understand everything before I dare do anything!" Any further learning must now be done on the job. No doubt the journeyman will make mistakes, but he can no longer blame his master or anyone else for what happens. He must pay the price of his mistakes himself.

As a ritualist, the journeyman tries to ensure that others are not affected by his own mistakes. He carries the cost himself. Self-responsibility is the discipline under which the journeyman grows. It has been said that a journeyman slips between two cracks in the fabric of society without distorting the tenor of its ways. He no longer lives in the same world as others. Much is real to him that is unregistered by others. He is in the world but not of it.

We know all this from our ordinary experience. When we use a doctor, architect, builder, shoemaker, or any craftsman, we expect them to do their job and make good any mistakes they may make. Just imagine your response to a dentist who explains a mistake by saying, "I'm sorry, but I wasn't trained very well"! What about a trained doctor who refuses to set up in practice? What a waste. This is recognition of the simple fact that greater knowledge and skill carry greater responsibility. As a journeyman ritualist, you should be able to respond correctly to any situation, to anger, fear, envy, or greed. Your own training should make it possible for you to recognize these.

.0As an apprentice, you will have become word-perfect in all the stages of ritual. The ritual gestures, the rules of the symbolic language, questions and answers, will all be familiar to you. However, as a journeyman, the significance of the gestures, words, and symbols deepen and the real import of them will begin to strike home. When the priest at the high point of the Mass raises the chalice, it should carry all the symbolic meaning that such an action can convey. It should be a moment of high emotion that has been built up by the whole ritual. St. Teresa of Avila reported that she once saw the Mass carried out by an unworthy priest and although the Host was surrounded by what she saw as devils, they were powerless to touch the Host itself. The Host remained an appropriate vessel to carry the influx of the divine. Similarly, when a bishop lays his hands on someone to be confirmed into the Church, or into the priesthood, there should also be a real influx of the Creative through the bishop in that person or priest.

Ritual provides a framework for power. Therein lies its strength. It allows power to be confined and channeled. It stops dissipation and creates the means to build up the power. People who participate in ritual will always vary in their strengths and powers. The value of a good ritual is that you can channel both weak and very powerful influxes within the same sequential structure. It is the task of the journeyman to build up the available power to a proper strength. Here he will have to exercise discrimination and some subtlety in handling the power with absolute precision in the execution of a ritual. To make the ritual a memorable experience requires not only precision but an element of art in manipulating the balance of the ritual. Such rituals linger in the memory as moments of sheer beauty. This too lies within the scope of a journeyman's work.

MORALITY AND KNOWLEDGE

The journeyman is still learning his trade. In this field, the journeyman is the one who knows that he does not know enough and that he is not perfect. This knowledge is not acquired through a sense of one's shortcomings in comparison with other people's talents, or from false modesty, but rather from an awakening of the moral sense within the individual. Morality is not a set of rules, a rigid list of rights and wrongs. Morality is the ability to know the fitness of things. The journeyman has awakened the moral sense within, and many things are registered by him that go unnoticed, but his morality is still not necessarily fixed or certain in its effects. Not everything he does is moral. Aware that he does not know, the journeyman must still act, and there is a fine difference here between acting from an awareness of one's limitations and acting by ignoring what one does not know. You can either cover up what you do not know or you can take responsibility for what you do, including the mistakes you make.

How does one train an individual to develop moral sense? It is clearly not a matter of learning a set of rules. Rules exist for those in whom the moral sense is not awake. If a child hits another child, the parent knows that it is not correct and makes it a rule for the child not to hit others. At the same time, one knows that children are like that and that the behavior is not actually immoral, but simply incorrect for people who have to live with their fellows. If that response is not checked, it will lead to a behavior pattern that will in time cause grief, both to others and to the child itself.

The methods used to train the moral sense are ritually important. At first, our approach is through ritual statements. One of the clearest examples of this is the Jesus Prayer or Prayer of the Heart, which is a simple statement: "Jesus Christ, Son of God, have mercy on me, a sinner." The prayer is repeated over and over in the middle of ordinary activities, during more formal times of prayer — the prayer should be repeated whenever the person remembers to do so. The apprentice stage of the prayer is the constant repetition of the words. In due course, the words, the verbal formulations, disappear and what is lodged in the heart is a wordless statement, which stays with one at all times. One can be more or less aware of this wordless statement lodged in the heart and one can trigger greater awareness of it through the words. This is the journeyman or meditative phase of the prayer. The wordless statement deepens and deepens into a wordless feeling and brings one to the threshold of what its meaning actually is. Here there are no words, no images. As this meditative phase progresses, the wordless feeling pierces deeper until there is nothing other than the contemplation of the prayer as reality. This is the stage of mastery. In another tradition, the phrases used are "The Lord giveth, and the Lord taketh away. Blessed be the name of the Lord," or "The Lord is in His holy temple. Let all the world keep silence before Him." Any ritual statement has three basic levels: the level of speech and image; the level of wordless feeling; and the level where it becomes reality and is contemplated as an entry to the Creative itself.

MASTERY

When you watch some sport, either live or on television, the impressive thing about someone who is a master of the game is not just the big points that are scored (which are impressive enough), but the seemingly casual, effortless accuracy of every move. When two great masters meet, in head-to-head conflict, you can see the mastery moving from one to the other as the game progresses. The casual scoring adds up, and as one master begins to dominate, the pressure builds up on the other until he has to raise his defenses to yet a higher level and he, the defender, begins to dominate. This is an example of "polarity switching," which escalates the game with mastery moving from one to the other and building up to the final crescendo. The atmosphere is charged.

In ritual, the raising of tension between male and female can lift the energy level to such a pitch that the air in the working space seems almost to be crackling with electricity. This is a situation of great potential and danger, and within the context of a male-female ritual, this danger is not unconnected with sex. One of the reasons for couples who are sexual partners in ordinary life not to act as priest and priestess in ritual is that the energy thus raised can be earthed very easily in familiar ways. Having received such a charge of power, one becomes very attractive to the opposite sex. In the immortal words of Henry Kissinger, "Power is the ultimate aphrodisiac"! Herein lies one of the great temptations for Eastern teachers who come to the West. In the East, social customs prevent too much contact with members of the opposite sex. In the West, such rules do not exist, and the powerful pull generated by the opposite sex in charged ritual atmospheres is easily succumbed to.

Mastery is the stage where right action is based not on feelings and thoughts about what should be done but on what is seen to be obviously the right thing to do. It is an instantaneous, effortless appreciation. There is no delay between the trigger and its response. The response, of course, could be either action or nonaction; indeed sometimes the most effective form of action is to do nothing. I remember how once, at a lecture, when the speaker invited questions from the audience, a person stood up and delivered a great diatribe on the whole subject. The speaker heard him out and said, "You think that, then?" "Yes!" exclaimed the person and promptly sat down. "Next question," said the speaker.

Mastery is the stage where morality is integrity. Integrity means wholeness; it is concerned with the essential rightness of each part of the whole and of the whole itself. What is the difference between a technically skilled pianist and a master of the art? Both can render the composition correctly enough, yet the master pianist adds a quality above that of the ordinary. This subtle quality has to do with integrity. Master engineers and builders, great artists and great mathematicians, have all been concerned with something they call beauty. Einstein, when shown some theory by an enthusiastic student, looked at it and commented, "How ugly!" Mathematicians in particular are attracted to solutions and theories that they label "elegant." What they are looking for is a beauty of form that has a quality of wholeness or integrity. This is also the quality that appeals to the moral sense. Mastery without morality is a contradiction in terms. Ritual must, in itself, be beautiful. It accords with the moral sense within us. It does not jar or grate upon our sense of wholeness. A mark of the growth of morality is that one turns away from the things that appeal to the worst in one, as a master craftsman will turn away from a bad piece of work. In the Old Testament, the highest quality under the Divine is wisdom, and the Hebrew word used for *wisdom* literally means freed of defect by the exercise of skill. The Book of Proverbs abounds in poetic descriptions of wisdom; here is one vivid passage, which sets out the relationship between the Lord and wisdom.

> The Lord created me at the beginning of his work,
> the first of his acts of old.
> Ages ago I was set up,
> at the first, before the beginning of the earth.
> When there were no depths I was brought forth,
> when there were no springs abounding with water.
> Before the mountains had been shaped,
> before the hills, I was brought forth;
> before he had made the earth with its fields,
> or the first of the dust of the world.
> When he established the heavens, I was there,
> when he drew a circle on the face of the deep,
> when he made firm the skies above,
> when he established the fountains of the deep,
> when he assigned to the sea its limit,
> so that the waters might not transgress his command,
> when he marked out the foundations of the earth,
> then I was beside him, like a master workman;
> and I was daily his delight,
> rejoicing before him always,
> rejoicing in his inhabited world
> and delighting in the sons of men. (Prov. 8:22–31)

Wisdom and understanding — one sees things for what they are and the other for the possibilities within. The mark

of mastery is a proper balance among knowledge, understanding, and wisdom. These three form the basis of correct
action. Great masters can be seen as those who by their
actions gave humanity a new and fruitful direction, who by
minimal action on their part gave birth to a vast movement
as the necessary response to their action. One of the great
Hebrew masters, Gamaliel, when asked about the authen-
ticity of the new Christian movement, said that if it was the
work of man, it would come to nothing; but if it was of
God, no man could overthrow it.

— CHAPTER SEVEN —

EMPOWERMENT

When the hand, the tool and the eye are one, that is one thing; when the mind and heart are engaged, that is another; but when the Creative enters, that is transcendence.

—Instructions to Members, Order of Sentinels

THE MAKING OF A TOOL IS ONE THING, CONSCIOUSNESS of it and knowledge of its nature another, the ability to use it creatively and appropriately is yet another. You have by now learned how to make tools. When they are all made and you are fairly satisfied with them (one should never be completely satisfied with appearances), then it is time to begin to know and appreciate them and their uses. Each tool summarizes a power and activity of intelligence. (Intelligence does not, of course, make one an intellectual!)

The process of knowing and being conscious of a tool is described as empowerment. In order to know one's tools intimately and to feel the power that will be channeled through them, two things are necessary. The first is to know the power contained in the instrument; the second is to know the power from which it derives its nature. The first has been put in it by its maker, while the second exists as a principle. The first is evoked and the second is invoked.

One can drive a car without knowing all that is in the car. You may know that it derives its power from its fuel, you may even know the principle of the internal combustion engine; but normally, that is all that is needed. Suppose you were actually aware of the powers of nature involved within the car. Suppose you remembered that all over the world others are using the same laws. Suppose you actually felt the ancient sources from which the fuel came, the millions of living creatures that were involved in its production and the awesome powers of the earth that combined to lay down these stores of fossil fuel. If you could feel this, all at once, as you were driving, then you would feel the sheer age and enormity of the principles involved. That feeling is empowerment.

The tools represent some of the underlying principles of our universe. Because they have material existence, all tools clothe the archetypal principle to which they pertain. No doubt the clothing would be different with a different understanding of the principles, but rather than get involved in comparisons between different systems, we will go through the set of clothing we are using, and leave the reader to compare and contrast it with more familiar systems.

EMPOWERING THE TOOLS

Having prepared the room and the working space in an appropriate manner, have all your instruments to hand. You should be dressed as simply as possible, with no adornments, bracelets, earrings, necklaces, rings, etc. You should have bathed and rinsed in clean water and have no makeup or any perfume on. You should be simply as you are. Cover the stone with the cloth. On the cloth, place the cup with fresh water in it. Put the sword on one side, the wand on the other. Take the cord and place it loosely around the stone.

The Wand

Sit comfortably and remember. Remember looking out into the night sky; if you don't remember, go out and do it. Then, remembering, start again. As you look out into the stars, you are looking out into the past of the universe. The further and smaller the specks of light, the further you are looking back into the past. The light traveling from that star started its journey years ago. In some cases, centuries or millennia will elapse before what is happening now in that place reaches here in the form of light, radiation of particles, and electromagnetic waves. When you look out over the earth at night, your eye may be attracted to a light somewhere. Between you and that light there is a straight line. What you see is a link, a link between appearance, attention, and the response within. That straight line is the wand.

When you point at something, a dog or a cat will look at your finger, but a person will look where you are pointing. A wand is an extension of attention: it links two things together. As a spear or an arrow, it flies from the thrower to the target. The wand can be used as a support or as a lever, and it can carry power from one place to another. Your wand is made up of two parts. One is for the transmission of energy and the other is for receiving energy. Make a distinction between the link and the power. The master wields the link. So the archetypal ruler of the wand is the Lord of Light, the transmitted light. The Lord is not the light itself, but he has power over it. The wand is not light; it is the transmitter of light. Think of it not as the generator of the laser beam but the beam itself. The beam shows up the path on which the light travels. This is the power in the wand. The wand is the power of direct connection.

Stand in front of your stone. Remove everything from its surface. Let it be clear. Visualize upon the stone a fire. Let that fire flame up and die down to glowing embers. Picture in your mind the process of starting up the fire using the bow you have made. It is the principle of the wand that transmits the power of the hand through the bow and its thread to the borehole with its shavings. Visualize clouds with rain falling from them into the cup you have made. The path of a raindrop, from cloud to cup, is the wand. See the wand itself. Raise it. Let it be a link between the light and the fire. Raise it again. Let it be a link between the clouds and the cup. Do not look at the light or the fire. Do not look at the clouds or the cup. Look at the wand. See and feel what it represents.

See and feel the power transmitted from every star to every star; from the sun to every point facing it on earth; from the sun to the moon; from the sun to every planet. See and feel the universe of light in which you live. Find words to describe this to yourself. Ask the wielder of that power to be present in your wand and in you. Find the wielder of that power within yourself. Let the wand connect that power outside you to that power within you. Do not do it wordlessly. By giving words to what you are doing, you will give form to the formless. You may think of the wording beforehand, if you like. But when you speak, let your intention be very clearly stated. If it makes you a little frightened, so much the better. One should fear the power of the Lord. When you have finished, wrap the wand in a fold of the cloth and set it aside.

The Stone

Next, standing before the stone, clear your mind of everything you have just done. See the stone — it is the working surface, it is the hearth, the oven, the chopping board, the chair, the floor, and the anvil of the smith. It is the principle that enables rocks to form and lava to flow in solid waves. It is the principle that enables men to build, placing one solid form upon another. It enables them to stand. It makes the forms of the crystals, builds the chemical elements. That same principle enables one pot of earth to grow a lily and a daffodil, a daisy and a geranium, a phlox and a miniature rose. The plants take what they need to form a plant whose flowers contain a triangle, a square, a pentagon, a hexagon, and a multipetaled flower; all are drawn from the elements of the earth. This power is not the earth itself; it is the intelligence that has dominion over it.

The stone is the archetypal form drawn from unsubstantial electrons, neutrons, and positrons to give reality and substance to us and our kind. It is the ground from which the earth springs. It is the great rock mountains devoid of life, which, when broken down by wind and ice, rain and heat, produce the luscious valleys in which life thrives. The stone, formed out of unsubstantial particles, possesses length, depth, height, and extension in time. It is the hearth where that great magician, the Lady of the Fields of Space, transforms wheat into bread or a hero into a tyrant. She draws out the shapes of nature. She hews out the suns, the planets with their satellites, the asteroids, the comets, the minerals. It is she with whom man works when manipulating these materials to form the plastics of our time. Remember, the Lady of the Fields of Space is not these things, but she has power over them.

Stand before the stone. Breathing lightly and easily, feel the weight of the stone, feel it in three dimensions, feel it in time. Go deeper into the stone, into the gaps between the grains of sand that make the rock. Still keeping the breath light and easy, visualize the grains as built up of little bits laid together randomly. Go further into even smaller bits that are like minute solar systems sharing planets. Feel the space between the bits. Feel the power that keeps them in position. Go as deep as your mind will let you, until you feel the stone as intangible forces holding one another in place. You may feel some contradiction between what you might see as tremendous motion and eternal stillness. Go towards the stillness. You have felt the stone.

Still standing in front of the stone, come back to your surroundings. First, see and feel where you are. Feel the depth of the solidity around you. Extend your vision to under your feet, to your left and to your right, in front and behind. Remain conscious of your breath. Extend your vision to the heavens above and to the space between the stars. Extend your vision in all the directions as far as you can go until you feel the immensity of space as a whole. This immensity lies within the stone and outside the stone. See the stone as representing all of this. Feel the stone as merely one point where the two, the outer and the inner, combine. If and when you feel this, let your breath fall to a minimum and hold the feeling on the outbreath. Stop and come back to ordinary vision.

Unwrap the wand. Hold it between the thumb and first two fingers. Recall the power of the stone and, again in words of your own choosing, request the presence of the Lady of the Field of Space in your stone. Let the heavier end of the wand represent the Lady's field of force; then, at precisely the moment when you finish your request, turn your hand over so that the heavier end is now pointing toward the stone. If, in the way you stand and in the balance of your body, you can feel that at the time of turning your hand over the balance is poised to change over so that it shifts from the weight of her field to the weight in the stone, so much the better. You will have charged and empowered the stone.

In the run of ordinary life it sometimes happens that you suddenly come to yourself in the midst of other things. Around you the air and atmosphere become crystalline, and at such times you feel that whatever you do next is important. This is the feeling of empowerment. An actor makes use of it: he gathers the attention of the audience from the hushed auditorium and begins. This also happens in a concert or at the opera, where the conductor waits for the hush to descend. Yes, we say *descend*, as though it comes from above. The conductor then raises his baton and the performance begins. The baton is his magic wand.

The Cup

Replace the wand in a fold of the cloth. Place the cup on the altar. The cup is the chalice, the grail, the container of life. It is the shape of liquid. It receives flowing liquid and also originates a flow. If you take a jug of water, you must raise the jug to a higher level in order for the water to flow into the cup. If there is difference, the flow will try to even out that difference. Rain falls onto a mountain. If there is a hollow, the water will fill the hollow, but otherwise it will of its own accord seek to escape, to run downhill, to join the sea. A trickle runs over the rocks, it joins other trickles, they form a stream. The stream joins other streams until they form small rivers and they run down to the sea. From small beginnings, it gathers momentum, building up power so as to join the sea.

The power of water to seek its own level is used to drive waterwheels and make electricity. It is the force that always tries to minimize itself by decreasing difference. The cup makes use of this force. The Lady of the Waters of Space governs the flows of all power that seeks to minimize itself. She is like the power of love, which seeks to join the lover and the beloved. She is like the power of the soul, which denies herself to join with her Creator. If you invoke the Lady of the Waters of Space, you invoke the urge to be one. You seek to minimize the gulf that stretches out between you and the other. However, where there is difference, there is also the urge to remain separate, to remain true to oneself. There is an inherent opposition to the joining, and she, the Lady, also balances these opposing forces. We have the urge to become part of the whole, to join in its oneness; we have the urge to be individual and join in *its* oneness. A hand is not a foot, but together they contribute to the oneness of the body. She is the power that governs this. She is the seed of life. If there were no difference between a man and a woman, why would they seek to come together? From this joining of one with the other, another difference is conceived. The child resembles both, yet is neither. Oneness and oneness join in the seed of another.

Life conjoins with life to produce life. Without life, processes run down. Life too runs down, but as it plays itself out, it begets more life, so by continual regeneration it never completely runs out. The chalice is a container of life. In most traditions, the chalice or cup is used in rituals of communion. The liquid within, whether it is sacramental wine, milk, or water, is blessed in an appropriate manner, and the act of drinking is the ritual acceptance of the greater life contained within the cup. Take up your cup. Feel it as a container of life. Feel it as a shape that will hold the shapeless.

Fill your cup with water. Empty the water out, and see how the water behaves. Refill your cup with fresh water and replace it on the altar. See the water as rain. See the trickles cover the rocks; see them join and make streams and rivers. Watch how the water is collected in reservoirs, pools, lakes, puddles. Follow the course of the water from reservoir to tap, from tap to cup. Follow the water back up to its source in the mountains. Follow the water going down into the drains and sewers, down into rivers and oceans. Follow and watch the transformation of the water into clouds that slowly drift into the colder regions of high mountains. Watch it transform back into rain. Feel the forms of life — the minerals eaten by plants, then returned into the ground once the plants have been eaten by living creatures, and broken down and collected by the roots of the plants, to nourish the life of plants once more. Extend your vision to the whole of life on earth, with all its forms, completing its ecological cycles.

Next you must make a leap of mind and feel that this process is not just happening on this earth, but is occurring wherever in the universe life exists. Viewed from the outside and speeded up many times, this solar system of ours would be seen to behave very like a living creature. If we could condense the movements of millions of years into a few minutes, the galaxy we live in, as it moves around the universe, would also look as though it were alive. If Jupiter continues on the path it appears to be taking, it could, given the right circumstances, turn into a solar system in its own right; then our solar system would have given birth to another.

Take out the wand. With the lighter end, point it above, point it below; point to the left and to the right; point in front and behind. Let the whole of life, from all the directions, flow through it into the cup. Put the wand away. Lift the cup to the heavens and in your own words ask that the Lady of the Waters of Space take up residence in your cup.

Remember, she is the commander of life. In times past, she was called Demeter, and when she went on strike there were no births, no fruits on the trees, no new seeds; there were no plants and nothing to harvest. She had withdrawn her command over the containers of life, and those that were living gradually began to die, as their stocks of food petered out. When she relented and consented to revivify the containers, everything resumed its original course, moving through cycles of life and death. Take the cup outside and pour the water on the ground while you remember what you are taking part in. You have now empowered the cup. Wrap it in a fold of the cloth.

The Cord

Place the cord upon the altar. The cord brings together many disparate threads of existence. Each thread remains indisputably itself, yet also joins with others to create a pattern that is larger than itself. The essential principle of the cord is that out of many strands of disorder, order appears. Pick up the cord. Hold it and feel its mutability. Look at the braiding, the triple threads tripled. Coil the cord on the altar in a figure of eight.

Within human beings, there are three main carriers of life that nurture and sustain the growth of the organism. We need air, water, and food; these are the strands of our life. These three primaries enter the human organism from outside it, each entering at its own rate. We have three liquid systems circulating within us — blood, lymph, and cerebrospinal fluid. We have a muscular system, which provides, transforms, and utilizes the energy from air and food and translates it into action through the brain and nervous system. This is of course an oversimplification, but it helps to show what the cord's "triple threads tripled" can mean.

The cord is the principle that coordinates the flow of each strand in such a manner that each strand maintains the existence of the other through a reciprocal arrangement. It is an ongoing process. It is the principle of interaction between living beings, or between a single living organism and its environment. Each organism affects the other in such a way that between them they maintain the form of the living being. This is the law of mutual maintenance.

Consider the plant kingdom on earth, which breathes out carbon dioxide when most other living creatures are asleep at night and which breathes in carbon dioxide when they are awake. Carbon dioxide and sunlight allow them to build up structures (and hence to grow) and store energy for themselves, so that at night, with no sunlight available, they break down structures and utilize the energy they have stored during the day. They don't, of course, use up *all* the energy they have stored; otherwise there would be no growth. Living creatures eat plants and so make use of the stored energy in plants for their own processes of growth.

Consider the plant kingdom as the lungs of the earth. The earth, spinning on its own axis, pumps the oxygen around the earth and the moon pushes and pulls all the liquids of the earth. The earth's movement around the sun shifts the seasons from northern to southern latitudes; the sun's heat pumps water to clouds and from clouds water falls back to earth again. Here is constant motion, flux, and change. Nothing stands still. Within the earth's biosphere, life nurtures life. It has its tides and its motions. He, the Lord of the Waters of Space, is the master of the tides, the master of the waves. Out of the chaos of the primordial waters swirl life and order. He commands order. It is no coincidence that milk poured into a wet sink resembles the design of galaxies and clusters of galaxies. Milk and the Milky Way follow a similar plan on vastly different scales.

In your mind's eye, move away from the earth and its tides and waves and consider the motions in deep space. As the solar system moves around the galaxy, it creates turbulence in interstellar gravity. The sun blasts its substance into space, but it also sweeps up into the solar system interstellar particles, which fall on the planets and the asteroids and comets and add to their bulk. The solar system feeds on the interstellar gas it attracts as it moves around the galaxy. As the experts tell us, the sun is a well of gravity into which things can sink. If you can see the three-dimensional ocean of space, you will notice that wherever there is a concentration of matter there is also gravity. Gravity keeps the planets in their courses. The planets are always being pulled into the sun, but because they are traveling at such high speed, they generate the force that pulls away from the sun, which exactly balances the attraction of the sun. The sun in its journey distorts the gravitational pressure of other starry entities. Space is not empty. Space has its streams, its lakes, its wells, its whirlpools. It is not chaotic, but it is a medium for constant motion. The Lord of the Waters of Space is master of those motions.

From the greatest to the smallest particle, the tides flow in complex strands. Take up the cord; feel its individual strands. Take out one thread and see the thousands of hairs that are twisted together to form it, each existent in its own right. See the separate threads, twisted together to form the cord. Extend your vision outward while holding the cord. Extend it to the earth around you and then to the heavens above. In words of your own choosing, call on the Lord of the Waters of Space to be present in your cord. Roll the cord around itself and place it in a fold of the cloth.

The Sword

Take up the sword. The sword is an extension of the tooth, the claw, the sting, the hand. It is related to the plow, the knife, and the chisel. The sword embodies the tool itself. Any tool increases skillful handling. You can break up vegetables, but it is simpler to cut them with a knife. A good tool also increases the power of its wielder. The sword is there to remind you that the power to make is the same as the power to destroy. The herb heals, but it can poison. The surgeon's knife can kill or cure. Alfred Nobel created dynamite to help save miners labor and found that it became a weapon. He felt so guilty that he created the Nobel Peace Prize. The Chinese used gunpowder to make loud noises at first and for entertainment. The discovery of atomic energy started off with scientific curiosity about investigating the power that was locked in the atom. What was the result? Hiroshima, Nagasaki, and Chernobyl. If you want life, you must have death; if you want power, you will have danger. If you ride in a car or a bus, you live with danger. If anything has the power to move you from place to place, it is inherently a dangerous weapon.

He, the Lord of the Fields of Space, is that from which all things are made. His scepter is the sword, with which he carves out space, making caves, mountains, and planets. He is lord of the power locked up in substance. The Greeks called him Hades, the Lord of the Underworld, and he was also called Pluto, the Rich One. His riches are all the minerals, crystals, and treasures that lie hidden underground waiting to be unearthed. He was a dark and brooding god who seldom left his domain. All that is living must descend into his kingdom to die and from there rise again in due season. The Lord of the Fields of Space is also the artist who wields the power to create a picture to please or terrify. A blank canvas has endless possibilities; the pots of paint hold within them infinite variations of color and form. He, the maker and the destroyer, limits the possibilities, defines the form. He wields the sword. Its cut, thrust, and parry define and limit. He is master of the borderlands in time and space. These are the edges — whether it is the line on the canvas or the edge between the known and unknown — they separate this from that, here from there, before from after.

The essential element of a sword is its sharpness; without this it is a sort of stick. A stick with an edge and a point can do different things from an ordinary stick. With the sword point you can make holes to plant seeds; with its edge you can hoe the ground and keep the weeds at bay and cut wood for fuel. You are the maker. You are the source of new things that can arise from the old. You are the destroyer. You are human, and you can make the laws of nature serve human purposes.

Lay the sword upon the stone, pointed away from you. Look at it and know that you can use it. Lift it to the heavens. Swing it downwards (don't hit yourself!). Carve a square in the air above the stone: using the sharp edge, cut across at head height, then cut down on both sides, and then cut a base. Keeping this square shape in mind, move around it and continue cutting until you have hewn a cube out of air. You have exercised a portion of the power that the Lord of the Fields of Space wields. Now, in all reverence, request his presence in your sword. You will know by the feeling of power in the sword whether or not it is empowered.

If you do not feel this power, replace the sword on the stone. Leave things alone until you feel it is right to pick up the sword and carve out the cube again. Do this however many times it is necessary, until you do begin to feel the charge and the power. To operate the sword as an instrument requires certainty and emotional power. Ladies sometimes find it difficult to take up this weapon with power and strength. (Don't tell anyone, but some men are afraid of it too!) When you finally feel that the sword has been empowered, wrap it up in the cloth with the other instruments.

The Cloth

You will now have all the instruments folded in the cloth. Place it, as it is, on the stone. The principle that the cloth embodies is the easiest to see but the most difficult to understand. It is a representation of the Lady of Light. It is the appearance of things, but the appearance is a clothing of the reality behind it.

When we look at anything, we see its appearance; we take that for granted. We see its physical properties. But what we see is based upon the operation of our senses. We are limited by the range of our vision, which ranges between violet and red. Those who are color-blind do not see the same colors and consequently live in a different world: the appearance of things is different for them. Those who are blind from birth "see" a different world again, and the same goes for people whose other senses are impaired. It is said, "You have never perceived the world in which you live, only the operation of your own senses." This is appearance. Each appearance is different, depending on the perceiver. None of them is the reality, but the fact that appearance differs for different people points the way to the reality, hidden and disguised by its clothing.

She, the Lady of Light, has sometimes been called Maya, the mistress of illusion. The Greeks called her Persephone or simply the Maiden, who returned every year in spring from the darkness of the underworld to the surface of the earth; her appearance was the new growth in living things. New buds emerge from the cold ground ready to burst into color and scent. The young and fertile celebrate her. She wields the power of desire. All the myriad forms that we see in creation — the clothing of the peacock, the serpent, the cuckoo in the nest — these are not what they seem. They are appearances of a hidden reality. They are deceptive. However, to quote Oscar Wilde, "It is only shallow people who do not judge by appearances." To perceive the forms of creation, we must, because we have no option, use the senses with which we have been provided in order to describe the reality that is hidden behind all we can perceive. It would be very easy to become cynical about the world if one realized in any depth that whatever one saw was illusory. But behind illusion is reality, hidden and disguised by its covering. Reality cannot be perceived as the appearance of things. However, without the appearance of things, one could not exist, one could not communicate with others, one would not even know that there were others in the world to communicate with!

As mistress of illusion, the Lady clothed in shimmering light shapes and illuminates. By wielding the power of desire, she creates appearances. The perceiver's desire enables him to participate in the world, to shape and mold it. One person wants things, so he fills his life with the appearances of things; another desires power and so becomes involved in the play of power; others want friends, so their lifestyle is concerned with people. All this may well be illusion, but it forms the basis of our lives.

The cloth covers, protects, and disguises whatever it contains. If you cover up a familiar object, you immediately see that by taking away from view its familiar physical properties you sense its underlying reality. If you take the cloth off again, you see its appearance. For a moment bring to mind all that you have ever seen. Extend your vision out to all that you can see. The infinitude of all those appearances is the principle of the cloth. Appearances that change from one moment to the next, appearances that continue for a length of time, seemingly unchanging: all these appearances, these forms of creation are like the cloth itself, covering and giving shape to the hidden reality of creation.

Your cloth, made of undyed threads, will appear to be the color of whatever colored light is shone on it. Lying with the objects enfolded in it, it takes on the shape of whatever it covers, and it will appear to be whatever shape that is. Ritual is an appearance, clothed in allegory and hidden in symbols. Behind ritual is reality. The cloth stands for the form of whatever ritual you may perform. Ask her, the Lady of Light, mistress of illusion and desire, to lend her reality to the operation of your work. See, in the weaving of your cloth, the appearance of form. When the cloth dances before your eyes, like a cinema screen showing a film of your desire, then the cloth has been empowered.

The Knife

We have not talked about the knife. It is the image and symbol of necessity. A simple description will suffice. Remember the saying "Necessity is the mother of invention." The knife is the Lord of Invention. You have already empowered it by using it to make all the other instruments.

CHAPTER EIGHT

WORLDS AND TRAVELERS

A world is complete in itself. Which world do you want to live in? Hell, Purgatory or Heaven?
—Instructions to Members, Order of Sentinels

OUR ORDINARY LIFE SEEMS FULL OF CONTRADICTIONS. Sometimes we are happy and our world is bright and expansive; at other times the world seems frighteningly dark and narrow. Mostly, the days are grey and inconsequential until some event jerks us out of our complacency. In this respect we are travelers moving from one world into another — worlds that are of our own making. One's field of awareness determines the size or actuality of one's world. Sometimes our world is small; at other times it is enlarged. When our world is larger, our field of awareness is greater and we seem to be living more intensely — as the old Chinese proverb puts it, "we live in interesting times"! Indeed one is no longer bored: everything has interest on all the levels.

In our normal life there are four different processes that operate within us at the same time. First, we receive impressions through all our senses from the world around us. These messages are collected, sorted, and sent to different parts in the brain. Normally we do not pay much attention to this process. What we are most aware of is the second process, which is the level of activity associated with pictures of ourselves. It triggers off an internal commentator which responds with "I like this," "I think that is very sensible," "I think that is very silly," or "I don't do that sort of thing, thank God!" and so on. This second process, which rumbles along all the time, can be distinguished from the other processes because it relates everything you become aware of (for example, all the different messages you receive through the senses) to some memory or attitude you hold. It is an endless chain whereby one thing reminds you of another and that brings to mind something else and that triggers off something else yet again, and on and on it goes. People have even written books based on observing this endless chain of associations, which is called "stream of consciousness" writing. Sometimes the chain loops back on itself and the process goes around in a circle like a mental roundabout. In the worst cases such a loop can lead to illness of mind, because the person cannot get off the roundabout.

The third process is more difficult to describe. It does not work with normal mental images or commentaries. The best way of describing it is to say that it concerns itself with meanings. The internal commentator shuts off and a sort of wordless thinking seems to take place. It is like when you have scrambled up a hill as fast as one can and, on reaching the top, you look up and the vista is vast and breathtaking. You drink it in; you observe without any words or feelings. (It is only when you come back down the hill and as you begin to talk to your friends about it that your associational level begins to work: "I liked that!") Sometimes it appears as though there is a watcher within who only observes what is taking place without passing any comment. The watcher also pops up into consciousness when there is something happening that we regard as important. In other words, it is a process that actually assesses the significance of what is happening, or its meaning.

There remains one other process left to describe. This manifests in what we perceive as a feeling of "being" or the sense of actually existing. This feeling of "being" does not break down into different descriptive parts of oneself, but comprehends a totality. It is the whole of one. Let us call this the operation of *psyche*. When the psyche or being level is operating, it comprehends the other three processes within the organism.

You can look at these four processes as different levels of operations and activities going on simultaneously within the human organism. They are organized like a pyramid that comprehends other pyramids within it. So, for example, the associational level includes the level of impressions; the watching level comprehends the associational level; and the being level comprehends all three of the others. It is only when one is physically awake that these processes occur simultaneously, and they are activated regardless of one's awareness; it is awareness that shifts and changes. The processes are interconnected and interrelated when one is awake, but during sleep their relationship changes and the connections between them break, so that they exist as discrete or separate worlds or levels of operation. Tests using hypnotic methods have shown how, during trance, every event or every impression (whether it is a sound, scent, a taste, a touch, or a shift in bodily posture) is registered in the memory of the hypnotized subject. We also know that the second level works when we are asleep, because the most common type of dream, with which we are all familiar, consists of associated images. These chains of association are triggered during our waking hours by impressions we receive from outside, but during sleep they are triggered by the internal activities of the brain. These dreams often take the form of a series of events that reflect the bustle of recent events that have happened to us.

A different type of dreaming exhibits the characteristics of the third level. The dreamer is in a state of deep sleep in which what is going on does not seem like dreaming so much as "thinking," and that is how subjects often describe it when they are woken up. If you are woken directly from this state of sleep (rather than passing through the second level on the way to waking up of your own accord), what remains is often a memory of great meaning — which, however, usually does not "mean" very much to the awakened mind. Finally there is the level of sleep where the "big dreams" take place, the ones that really do have the marks of strength and depth of meaning.

These four processes or levels have also been described by those who have had near-death experiences. First, the ordinary senses seem to close down and external impressions become meaningless; then the sense of self-identity fades. The next level to go is the thinking process, with a consequent alteration in the sense of time and place. Finally, a stage of great power appears which often recapitulates the person's religious beliefs. In some cases this stage may be accompanied by an apparent view of one's own corpse from outside and above the body, and one may seem to be offered the choice of returning to the body or leaving it completely. (In other cases, the body itself seems able to call back this detached spirit or viewpoint.) This is the operation of the level we have called psyche.

Over the millennia people have been fascinated by the possibility of carrying the ego or "sense of I" through the gates of death. Methods have been evolved for attempting to separate the "spirit" from the "body," despite the fact that they obviously coincide. There are three main works extant on this subject: *The Egyptian Book of the Dead, The Tibetan Book of the Dead,* and Frances Dalton's *Book of the Art of Dying.* A particular method used in clairvoyant circles is described in the works of Muldoon and Carrington (such as *The Projection of the Astral Body*), who tried to order the different ways used for separating the being from the body. Most of these methods are too dangerous to practice from instructions in a book, and in fact none of them should be practiced except under supervision from someone who has personally gone through the process.

WHO SAYS WHAT?

In ritual work one makes use of these four different processes or levels of operation. In theory, there are also two higher levels, but we can only talk about what is within the experience of most people in the course of ordinary life. One might suppose that the associational level is not useful for ritual. But the internal commentator is the mechanism that internalizes that which is outside the organism and similarly externalizes the internal worlds and attitudes that one holds. This mechanism interprets and translates the situation in terms of the picture one has of oneself. In many systems of thought this level — the "I" or ego level — is considered to be a hindrance for the full development of human potential. What, however, is the role of the "I"? The "I" is a hindrance only if it is allowed to rule in such a way that stops an awareness of the other processes, like the watching level, which occur within the organism. The "I" is a good steward but a bad master. What we perceive through the medium of the watcher or of psyche has to be interpreted through the "I." The "I" is ruler, therefore, of the means of communication available to us. Language belongs to this level of association, as does our store of words, images, and labels from which we draw to communicate our experience. What the watcher or the psyche perceives is interpreted by the "I" and clothed in familiar words and images. If the "I" is incapable of doing that, then those perceptions remain simply as unformulated feelings and inchoate experiences.

Inability to communicate or speak about such experiences isn't much use in ritual work when you are working with others. If you cannot respond to their signals in a constructive way, how can you work together? The "I" must use language to externalize inner perceptions. But what normally happens is that we cling tightly to a certain picture of ourselves and do not admit anything that does not perpetuate this picture. The "I" edits all the information and impressions we receive, from either inside or outside, in such a way as to bolster this picture. This leads to unconscious lying about what is being perceived, and then we are well and truly caught in the mesh of self-deception. A lying "I" is not much use as interpreter of events and experiences. So the "I" must submit to a master, a source of reference other than itself. You will have noticed that in the making of the instruments the instruction was to stop work every time your attention wandered and to open up your senses. Getting caught up in your favorite daydream is a good example of the "I" reinforcing your picture of yourself. Opening up the senses allows new information to enter. This helps disentangle the "I" from its favorite pastime by turning its attention to the new information, which has to be organized. The "I" is then acting as an interpreter, which is its proper role; it is allowing external impressions to enter the internal world. All our knowledge about the external world enters through the medium of the "I" or ego level, and without it no action in the external world is possible.

Let us now turn to the process of watching. We have already said that the activity of this process seems to involve a wordless thinking. The watcher observes without passing comment. This ability presupposes a state of detachment that is unfamiliar to the "I," which is much more involved in the hurly-burly of getting things done. The ability to watch without comment allows a different range of perception to come into being. Sometimes the watcher can observe events and see the longer-term consequences of actions and events. This is well within ordinary experience: sometimes you suddenly know that something "important" is happening: it could simply be a conversation with someone or a chance meeting with a stranger. At the time you are unable to formulate what you are sensing, but eventually it may filter through to your associational level as a stray thought, perhaps, or an intuition or a dream. When the event takes place that "proves" this — say the stranger many years later becomes a partner in some project — one's reaction is usually "I knew this would happen" or "I had a strange feeling about this!" The watcher, at that original meeting, had foreseen the consequences; the stray thought or intuition reminds us of what it had seen then, when we probably ignored it.

At other times, the watcher acts as a guardian at the threshold of consciousness. It is like an alert sentry that observes things coming and going and stops anything that does not have the right password, so to speak. In ritual work it is, therefore, necessary to have such a password, which could take the form of the right attitude or a symbolic language. In the terms of the four processes, the watcher does not allow the level of words and images to enter into its world. This works the other way as well. The formless activity of the psyche will not be allowed to pass through into ordinary consciousness if the "I" is unprepared to meet it by giving it appropriate clothing. In this sense, the watcher maintains the integrity of the being by preventing any dangerous influx of power. Alarm bells are rung. But the scope of the watcher is limited by the particular time and place in which it is operating, and by the structure of the human organism.

The psyche is the individual's sense of being. It holds together all the bits and pieces of the whole being as a seamless garment; in this sense it is operative all the time, however entangled one's consciousness is in the "I." You may have had the experience of meeting someone you used to know thirty years ago, and still recognizing him or her: however much a person's external appearance changes, with age or with fashion, their psyche does not change.

The field of awareness of psyche has a scope that breaks the boundaries of time and place. The psyche can become conscious of other entities that have a similar nature, entities that can resonate with the human archetype. The psyche is a stranger in a strange world — stranger than fiction but surer than fact.

INTO THE LIGHT

In ritual work, these four different processes are used according to the purpose at hand. Most divination methods depend on the "I" falling into a passive state so that the watching process is emphasized. In taking a passive role, the "I" performs only as requested. It should not volunteer any information or edit what has been seen. If, however, you wish to divine and investigate at the level of the psyche, then even the watcher must become passive and cease to perform its usual practice of guarding the threshold of consciousness. The simplest way of elucidating how this type of ritual can be set up and operated is by giving an example.

Assume that the purpose of the ritual is to acquire information about some matter far in the past. As this is an investigation at the level of the psyche, we would have a traveler representing the psyche, who, as it were, goes out into the strange country. Another person would perform the function of the watcher by guarding the consciousness of the ritual lodge or working space. Another person would act as an interrogator or the "I" by asking relevant questions of the traveler.

As always, you will first need to invite the appropriate guardians to the four quarters. Since the matter is to do with the past, it concerns the Lord and Lady of the Fields of Space, so the Lords and Ladies of Light and the Waters of Space will act as guardians of the four quarters. The Lady of the Fields of Space is placed as the receptive and is evoked while the Lord of the Fields of Space is invoked. Their tools, the sword and the stone, will therefore be used and are placed together in the working space.

The traveler is seated behind the stone. The person who acts as watcher takes up the sword and, holding it upright, sits in front of the stone. The interrogator faces the watcher. The psyche falls into a meditative and contemplative state. The watcher extends his or her perception to the whole space and tries to maintain its integrity. The interrogator begins the proceedings by asking the psyche questions.

> **Interrogator:** Go to somewhere in the past. (Leaves time for this to happen.) Where are you?
> (Psyche answers as he is able. It often happens that speech becomes difficult for psyche, and the questioner has to wait for the words to come out.)
> **Psyche:** On a hill.
> **Interrogator:** What can you see in front of you?
> **Psyche:** Another hill.
> **Interrogator:** How are you dressed?
> **Psyche:** As usual.
> **Interrogator:** What do you have on your feet?

Psyche: Nothing.
Interrogator: What do you have on your head?
Psyche: A circlet.
Interrogator: What sort of circlet?
Psyche: A round one.
Interrogator: What is it made of?
Psyche: Copper.
Interrogator: Is there any decoration on it?
Psyche: Yes.
Interrogator: What sort of decoration?
Psyche: Copper leaves.
Interrogator: Are you clothed?
Psyche: Yes.
Interrogator: What are you wearing?
Psyche: A robe.
Interrogator: Anything else?
Psyche: Yes.
Interrogator: Is it a cloak?
Psyche: No.
Interrogator: Is it a coat?
Psyche: Yes.
Interrogator: Is it a long one?
Psyche: No.
Interrogator: How far does it reach?
Psyche: To my thighs.
Interrogator: What is it made of?
Psyche: Wool.
Interrogator: Is it colored?
Psyche: Yes.
Interrogator: What color is it?
Psyche: Green.
Interrogator: Where is the sun?
Psyche: Behind me.
Interrogator: Is it high in the sky?

Psyche: Yes.
Interrogator: Is it at its highest?
Psyche: No.
Interrogator: Is it still rising?
Psyche: Yes.
Interrogator: Is it nearly at its highest?
Psyche: Yes.
Interrogator: Is it directly behind you?
Psyche: No.
Interrogator: Is it behind your left?
Psyche: No.
Interrogator: Is it early in the year?
Psyche: No.
Interrogator: Is it late in the year?
Psyche: No.
Interrogator: Is it midsummer?
Psyche: Yes.
Interrogator: Why are you standing there?
Psyche: I am waiting.
Interrogator: Why are you waiting?
Psyche: I have been asked to.
Interrogator: For what reason?
Psyche: To meet a man.
Interrogator: Why should you meet this man?
Psyche: To take him to the priestess.
Interrogator: What is in the valley?
Psyche: The house of the priestess.
Interrogator: What is the house made of?
Psyche: Stone.
Interrogator: What sort of stone?
Psyche: Stone from the hill.
Interrogator: Which hill?
Psyche: The one I am standing on.
Interrogator: Are the stones squared?

Psyche: No.

Interrogator: What is between the stones?

Psyche: Moss and clay.

Interrogator: Do you have anything in your hand?

Psyche: Yes.

Interrogator: What is it?

Psyche: My staff.

Interrogator: What is the staff made of?

Psyche: Wood.

Interrogator: What sort of wood?

Psyche: Alderwood.

Interrogator: Why is it alder?

Psyche: That is my mark.

Interrogator: Has the man come yet?

Psyche: Yes.

Interrogator: What are you doing now?

Psyche: I am leading him down the hill.

Interrogator: Which direction did he come from?

Psyche: My right.

Interrogator: Where did he come from?

Psyche: From the circle.

Interrogator: What is the circle?

Psyche: It is where we meet.

Interrogator: When do you meet?

Psyche: In the spring.

Interrogator: Where is the sea?

Psyche: All around.

Interrogator: How far away?

Psyche: Two days, six days.

Interrogator: Days of walking?

Psyche: Yes.

Interrogator: How many days to the circle?

Psyche: Two days.

Interrogator: Does the man carry a weapon?

Psyche: Yes.
Interrogator: Is it iron?
Psyche: What is iron?
Interrogator: Is it brown?
Psyche: Yes.
Interrogator: Is it a sword?
Psyche: Yes.
Interrogator: Does he carry something else?
Psyche: Yes.
Interrogator: What is it?
Psyche: Wood words.
Interrogator: Is it for the priestess?
Psyche: Yes.

I shall not continue. The main points of the inquiry have become plain. The ritual should be closed down in the proper manner, and the guardians thanked and asked to leave. As to the information gathered from the investigation, psyche does not know of iron but does know copper. The sword is probably made of bronze. Psyche is facing north by northeast. The man is coming from east-southeast. It is summer and it is nearly noon. The place is an island and, judging from what has been said, probably a large island. If we assume that twenty-five miles a day is a reasonable walking distance for somebody used to it, the island could be about 125 miles long at its longest point.

Note that psyche does not volunteer answers and does not explain. The interrogator has to get all the information by direct questions. The more precise the question, the more informative the reply. This is a long process, and there should be a scribe to note down all the answers and to sketch the geography of the place. From the answers given so far, the island is quite far north. You could elicit the exact location by asking questions about the length of days, but that might prove very difficult. Perhaps a line of questioning about how far you could walk before sunset would be more useful. The watcher should also report to the scribe afterwards about the quality present in the working space, and especially at what points in the questioning the feelings in the space changed. Such a session could take quite a long time and the interrogator must be skilled at the task.

Another method can be used, but it is not as reliable or consistent. The stone and the sword would be used as before, but this time the watcher would be the respondent, the "I" would be the interrogator, and psyche would take on the task of maintaining the spatial integrity by simply keeping the balance. In this ritual, the watcher would have to be given precise clues to work from, rather than a free choice of what to answer. He would need keys to home in on a specific time and place; this can be done by giving a specific symbol, scent, and mix of colors. The watcher should be placed in front of the stone from the beginning. The interrogator would have to lead the watcher by describing the surroundings, and by presenting changes in them. He would have to ask leading questions such as "Why is the person in front of you wearing a rose?" and "A man has come to give you something. What is it?" Such leading questions make the whole procedure much more constrained and dependent on the preconceptions of the interrogator and the thoughts and feelings of the watcher. The person acting as psyche also has a far more difficult task in keeping the balance because of the subjectivity of the watcher and the interrogator.

If the watcher is allowed to have an even freer hand in commenting on what he or she perceives, then the operation will resemble a séance. The popular portrayal of séances is not particularly accurate: it is not necessary to hold hands, to be in darkness, or to have background music. But a séance will of necessity be concerned not with the sword and stone but with the cloth and wand. Here the risks for self-deception are great, as the process is extremely subjective. In séances, hearing is usually the main factor, so words acquire great importance, and, as we have already pointed out, words and language belong to the associative level. Words have different connotations for different people and as such are subject to different interpretations both by the speakers and the hearers. Verbose answers should always be noted and any inconsistencies followed up. As in any ritual method, the important factor is the theoretical structure that is held in common by the group. Is there a shared understanding? A common vocabulary?

DREAMTIME

Another method for acquiring information and for divining is to put the operator into a light sleep and let him or her dream. This method needs great experience and control on the part of the operator. Control of dreams can be achieved, but only after a long course of training. The method used is usually a variant based on the principle of "remembering the day." Before going to sleep at night, every night, the operator should go through the experiences of the day in reverse order, starting with getting into bed, and continuing back right through to the moment of waking up. This should be done until the dreamer is able to be awake while dreaming. It may take years to achieve this state. At first the process will send the operator to sleep; then it will shift to a state where there is great influx of energy, which effectively *prevents* the operator from going to sleep. At this point, minimal breathing should be practiced. Start with a very long inbreath, followed by a very long outbreath. Then, by gradually withdrawing the element of effort from the long breaths, the breath can become very light and the body becomes very calm and quiet. It is then quite easy to slip into sleep, but while the breath is at a minimum, a quiet instruction should be given — "Mind, remember" — and then one should slip into sleep. On waking up, the operator should write down whatever is remembered from the night before.

No attempt should be made to analyze the remembered dreams. They should be noted down without commentary. The dream is the message in exactly the same way as a painting is the artist's message. If the artist could have communicated his message in any other way, there would have been no need to paint the picture. The process is very similar with dreams. Unfortunately the associative mind always wants explanations, and that very often destroys the meaning content. As most people have discovered, explaining an experience of deep feeling can do it to death. When critics explain every single connotation and syntactical structure and mood of a poem, what are we left with? When the logical and associative mind gets to work, it removes all the meaning content and we are left with only ashes in the mouth. Logic is, after all, only one particular way of arriving at a conclusion, and often the path logic chooses leads not to truth but to a conclusion that we actually desired to reach in the first place.

Most trance states are achieved by cutting the connection to the level of impressions. This level is involved with the survival of the organism, since we can react appropriately to external impressions of which we are aware. The impressions received by our senses are organized in the brain. This occurs automatically and we do not pay much attention to it (which is a good thing, because if we interfered with it, we could cause a lot of damage to the organism). In a trance state, people have been known to perform extraordinary feats of bodily endurance. By cutting the channel between sensory input and organization in the brain, normal bodily reactions are curtailed so that people can be pierced with swords, they can be cut without any blood flowing, or they can walk over hot coals without being blistered or burnt. The shaman makes use of two separate levels — that of impressions and that of the psyche. It is not easy to be trained as a shaman. They say that every shaman has died and his parts have been scattered throughout the world of the living and the dead. A shamanic tradition often trains its practitioners to become one in mind and feeling with an animal. They identify with an individual animal and thus with the whole of that species.

In ordinary life we cannot, of course, undergo such ordeals. However, what we do know from the science of today is that human beings have a unique structure upon which our physical bodies and physical characteristics are built. This structure, known as DNA, consists of a very complex chain of molecules whose basic building blocks are present in most living animals on the planet today. It requires no great stretch of the mind to suppose that if we could, by some activity of the mind, feel the operation of these building blocks within ourselves, we would be in a position to contact the other species who share the same building blocks. It is at this molecular level that a connection can be made, and obviously, in penetrating to such physical and instinctive depths, our normal language of words and feelings would be incapable of expressing the experience. Our descriptions are based on *human* sensory perception, so that whatever experience we might share with another species would be difficult to translate into a human context. However, the principle can be clearly seen even in ordinary life, as there are some people who naturally have a strong rapport with certain animals and are in turn trusted by them. This is very obvious in the case of the dog lover and the horseman.

Each of us has his or her own world with its own specific internal structure: we create words and images in order to handle the things that happen to us. So each world is only partially equivalent to someone else's world, but at the same time as human beings we share a common basis. This is the source of our creativity — that we are both the same and different from other people.

Things can affect other things only if they possess a common structure and sensitivity to change. This principle is best illustrated by music. If two stringed instruments are tuned to exactly the same notes, a note sounded on one instrument will result in the same note being sounded by the other (provided, of course, that they are not too far apart). Most people physically hear the same notes and harmonies, but this does not mean they always respond in the same way in translating what they have heard into words and images. So a piece of music may have evoked similar emotional responses in every member of the audience, but each person may well put a different quality on it. If the emotional response is a yearning, some people might consider that a beautiful emotion, while for others it may be a hurtful emotion, one to be avoided. The experience is common; the judgment on it is not.

Differences of interpretation lead to arguments, and arguments lead to futile strife. If we wish to communicate directly with another person, we have to do so at a level more primitive than words or images. An example of such direct communication in which we almost all participate is the sexual act. The mother of a newborn baby also communicates at this primitive level with the baby: her responses to the baby's needs are preverbal. However, it is also possible to communicate precisely through words, images, and feelings, as long as the directness of the primitive level is harnessed and not lost. In ritual work this is exactly what happens. If people are trained in a ritual over a period of time, then by constantly repeating that ritual, an agreed vocabulary of feelings and images coheres in the group. This then enables the participants to communicate on some very specific matter through controlled and exact feelings.

BLACK AND WHITE

We have spent some considerable time discussing the four processes that occur, how they may be recognized, and what they organize. We have seen them within our ordinary consciousness, as well as our states of sleep and dreaming, and we have indicated how these processes can be utilized in ritual work. We have not, however, directly said much about the familiar state of daydreaming. This occurs when the ego or "I" cuts itself off from both the higher and lower levels. Daydreams (and nighttime dreams of the same kind) are particular to each person's private world and are caused by the self-importance of "I." These dreams are based on pictures of oneself — pictures of self-glorification or self-punishment. They are expressed in films like *The Secret Life of Walter Mitty* and *Billy Liar*.

We all have dreams that are more than reflections of an inner fantasy world, however. We can dream about a possible future, a dream that is a true reflection of the inherent capabilities of a human being. These dreams could have to do with our personal purpose in life and our immediate environment, or they could be concerned with the culture and society we live in. Martin Luther King had a dream. Many a thinker has dreamt a utopia. These dreams are not simply vague idealism, but rather visions of what is possible.

There are dreams that are based on understanding and knowledge. For the individual, if they are remembered, they can instruct the conscious "I" on matters that could be important for growth. Many works of art perform this function for mankind at large. Such works of art are, as it were, dreams at the level of mankind itself. It could be said that Newton dreamt the eighteenth- and nineteenth-century world of science into existence. Einstein picked up this same dream and furthered it; and later America and Russia realized it and carried the dream out into space.

Dreams based on wisdom and creativity are of an even higher order. Such dreams will, if the time and conditions are right, point out a new and fruitful direction for the development of the human race. Such dreams have been dreamt by people such as Moses, Krishna, Buddha, Lao Tse, Confucius, Zoroaster, Socrates, Christ Jesus, Mohammed, Guru Nanak, Baha'ullah. The list is, we hope, endless. The particular visions may vary enormously, but at this level they always enrich human potentiality. The visions may or may not be divine; you will regard them as divine if that is how you have been brought up. This is not meant to be controversial. Rather it is meant to show how the highest level of vision, if it can be translated in such a way that the ordinary mind or "I" of each person can appreciate it to some degree, can lift the ordinary mind to the greater world in which it lives. We cannot lay down any method for attaining to this level of comprehension.

What *is* within the grasp of most people, however, is the same level of dreaming and vision that great artists, scientists, architects, and so on can reach. A traditional method to achieve this level of vision is by scrying. Here again there are many different systems that have been used over the years, but the essential part of this method is that it is a means of perceiving a greater world. Any reader who lives in or passes through London might find it worthwhile to visit the Museum of Mankind, where there is on display a human skull carved out of rock crystal. If you look through the eyeholes of this skull, you can see a much greater world. One can see clouds of dark and light and formations of stars and galaxies stretching out into the depths of space. It is rather like looking out onto a very clear night, with no moon, no clouds, and no interference from any source of light. I am told (though I have never seen it personally) that the night sky in a large desert has the same quality. Does this account for the number of prophets who have come out of the desert?

A crystal ball has the same characteristic and is the traditional tool for scrying. Many people use a glass ball, but this is not recommended unless the glass contains many small bubbles. The evenness of glass does not evoke the right level within oneself. Another system, used especially for exploration of the past, is gazing into a pool of ink. The ink has a depth of blackness with the occasional sheen of light, which evokes within a sense of gazing at the very beginning of creation. Yet another method is to fill a bowl with water and add a few very small drops of oil. The way the drops of oil move, join together, and separate echoes the processes in creation. These three methods evoke in the perceiver different aspects of the creation of the universe. Without taking this too seriously, one could say that the Lady of Light, the Lady of the Fields of Space, and the Lady of the Waters of Space were each involved with one of these methods. However, these methods do have one quality in common, in that they remind us of the starry world; hence such activities have often been called "astral travel."

Ritual societies have their own methods of training. If one is willing to submit to their rules, they will instruct people in such practices at the appropriate time. Unsupervised or accidental development of such activities has occasionally led to serious mental illness. This is caused by the apparent reality of such experiences and the complete incomprehension by others of the nature of such experiences, leading to a progressive alienation from the society in which the person lives. It is the alienation that is the illness, *not* the experience. This is very clearly argued by Paul in the New Testament, where he discusses the subject of glossolalia — the gift of tongues or the speaking in unknown languages:

> Follow after love, and desire spiritual gifts, but rather that ye may prophesy. For he that speaketh in an unknown tongue speaketh not unto men, but unto God: for no man understandeth him; howbeit in the spirit he speaketh mysteries. But he that prophesieth speaketh unto men to edification, and exhortation, and comfort. . . . Now, brethren, if I come unto you speaking with tongues, what shall I profit you, except I shall speak to you either by revelation, or by knowledge, or by prophesying, or by doctrine? . . . If any man speak in an unknown tongue, let it be by two, or at the most by three, and that by turn; and let one interpret. But if there be no interpreter, let him keep silence in the church; and let him speak to himself, and to God. Let the prophets speak two or three, and let the other judge. (1 Cor. 14:1–3, 6, 27–29)

This chapter has dealt with how we may perceive the imperceptible. There are many different methods of doing this, but they involve the same faculties of the human being. Paul describes these as "spiritual gifts" and in 1 Corinthians 12 he deals with how there are "diversities of gifts, but the same spirit"; how there are "differences of administration but the same Lord" and further how there are "diversities of operations, but the same God." As with glossolalia, which Paul exhorts his readers to use to edify the church or to teach others, here he emphasizes the importance of gifts being "given to every man to profit withal." Which brings us to a crucial question: what use do we make of that which has been perceived? The next chapter will consider why we practice the methods that allow us to perceive the imperceptible. Why do it at all? Should we know everything that there is to be known? What use do we make of any new information? Should an astrologer say that she or he sees death in a horoscope? Another point of view is illustrated proverbs such as "Let the past bury the past," "Let sleeping dogs lie," and "Speak only good of the dead."

CHAPTER NINE

SURVIVAL

Life competes with entropy by perpetuating itself,
generation unto generation.

—Instructions to Members, Order of Sentinels

I N THE ANIMAL KINGDOM, SURVIVAL OF THE SPECIES IS paramount. From the evidence that we have gathered on species that are now dwindling on earth, it also seems that some creatures require a "community" of a minimum size for their perpetuation. Once the "community" drops below a critical number, then the species loses its will to survive. In human communities this principle also holds true. The history of the Jews, Parsis, and Armenians suggests that they require a critical number in order to survive as a community within another culture. I have chosen these particular groups as they are easily distinguishable from other minority groups and have historical records. The Jews in Bihar, India, died out, as the Cornish language died out in England. In both cases, the community lost faith and confidence in itself and its own continuity.

Animals have three major instinctive responses to danger and the unknown. They either fight to gain supremacy or they flee to avoid the danger or they freeze and submit to the superior force. These three are the basic drives in animals, and all other responses are either simple reflexes or conditioned responses to situations. Success for a hunter depends on separating an individual from the herd. The most curious thing is that once the individual animal has been killed by the hunter, the rest of the herd seem to go about their business quite unconcerned. It is almost as if the animal who alerts the herd has to fight the hunter; then, regardless of who the winner is, the herd knows that it is safe. It is different if the herd is hunted by a pack of killers, like the killer dogs in the Deccan in India. Safety then lies not in crowding together but in scattering.

The various strategies adopted by nature to protect a species have their counterparts in human activity. Individuals can certainly subordinate their will to the "herd," with consequent similarity of behavior. This subordination appears to take place on different levels. At all levels, however, if a person sticks out like a sore thumb and does not conform to the standards of the group, group dynamics will take over and the person will eventually be rejected. There is the gang or clique, and at a different level there is the mob. In the British army you hear people saying, "Our mob is the best," which is an innate recognition of the identity of this type of grouping. Then there is a city with all its inhabitants and sets of inhabitants; and a city exists within a country.

This is true of any town, city, or region where the smaller groups or entities live within the greater entity. The smaller gains greater cohesion by being subordinate to the larger. Some countries are more prone to it than others. Britain has been called a nation of clubmen, because most British people belong to some small "elite" or another, whether it is the elite of the local pub, or that of Latin speakers, or that of bingo players.

In a well-structured society, there are numerous entities, and individuals identify with several at once. As individuals, we are part of a family, and we may also belong to the local cricket club or be enthusiastic members of a church or local council. These small entities live within the great entities of town, city, county, or region. Regional

identity is very strong in some areas, and identifying someone's region from their speech is part of the ritual of recognition in Britain. Where a region has two major elites of
equal power and influence, then trouble is bound to start.
Each is too big to be ignored by the whole. Because they are
so large, they must battle to determine which will become
the regional identity. In the last resort, this leads to civil
war, and the victor who has won outright wins the prize of
giving the region its identity.

We can see this in familiar circumstances. When matters get to this stage the only possibilities are to fight to the
death, to leave the arena, or to freeze and thereby submit to
the entity that has gained control. When Henry VIII's
authority was challenged by the Church of his time, he had
no option (if he wanted to remain king) but to vanquish the
Church leaders who owed their allegiance to Rome. Most
entities on the same level of power battle to gain precedence, and many rituals have been designed to allow these
entities to exist provided they do not threaten the existence
of the greater entity.

RITUAL BATTLES

It has been said that the Anglo-Saxon race keep a tight rein
on their emotions because they are a violent people and the
violence lurks just below the surface. As a consequence, the
British have created arenas where "ritual battles" can take
place. The ritualistic mode ensures the presence of certain
checks and balances that are vital if people are to govern
and control themselves. Our law courts are battlegrounds
between defense and prosecution. Our parliamentary
House of Commons is an arena where government and
loyal opposition fight out the question of who will rule and
how they will rule. The House of Lords and the House of

Commons fight out their prescribed roles. The police and judiciary do not normally cooperate; a magistrate's court is effectively a people's court. Magistrates are not lawyers, but are drawn from the ranks of the public, so that this battle takes place between the public and the offender. The different aspects of our society battle together so that something viable for the whole is created. Any highly structured society has within it warring elements that interact in specific ways to maintain the greater whole. If an element is victorious to the degree that it challenges the existing order and becomes the status quo, then we witness a major change in the fabric of society.

For changes to take place, for any organism to reorganize itself, there has to be a structure that is commonly accepted by the different aspects of the organism; in this instance, society itself is the common ground. The structure is usually complex, but fundamentally it rests on the fact that we are all human beings and share similar faculties. Humans organize themselves quite differently from animals, despite our similarities with the animal kingdom. Most of the faculties in animals operate instinctively, that is to say, they operate automatically because these drives are preprogrammed into their system from the beginning. However, as has been said before, because we humans have a conscious commentator, many of our abilities are self-programmed or learned from others. For instance, we can communicate and do so very precisely. Our capacity for speech and precise communication over a wide range of activities requires a commonly accepted structure — that is, language. The capacity for language is shared, but different languages develop according to the needs of the people and specialize in matters that are important to the users. For instance, Eskimos have well over thirty words to describe snow: they need them to survive. Spanish is rich in adjectives, Arabic in overtones of meaning (which make it a natural language for poetry).

Some languages specialize in the rational. Many so-called "primitive" societies specialize in the effects of the unseen worlds. Their languages deal with a life in which one is surrounded by unseen forces. But we all live in a world of unseen forces; it is just that in the modern West we have given these forces scientific instead of personal names and explained their action in scientific terms. We rationalize their existence. In the final analysis, our scientific culture is but one specialization of human endeavor. The scientific myth is our reality. This does not mean that as a myth it has no validity, but rather that all such specialized myths serve as models for the society in which people live. They are not just abstract or emotional models, but practical ones which govern the life of the people. We weigh and measure, assign time and place. Others did the same in their own way. The world of the Middle Ages was one in which angels and devils had reality for people. The Egyptians created a science of death. To them, the gods and images of the other life were real: witness the time and wealth they spent on building their tombs. Nowadays, in the field of economics, there is a process known as specialization-simplification-standardization. Since the eighteenth century we have specialized in reason and logic; having simplified the reasoning process, we have now come toward the end of that sequence by the creation of logic machines. We have created the computer and eventually computers will be standardized.

By establishing certain basic principles upon which we base our knowledge and beliefs, we create worldviews and organize society. But that initial choice we make is an emotional one. There seems to be no good reason that one chooses one path rather than another. Having established our basis, we organize experience around it and conduct our battles within its framework. We might modify the basis slightly through the fruits of our experience, but there comes a time when we can no longer keep modifying our basis. We then change the status quo completely to one we are happier with. Again, this is an emotional choice.

Let us develop this a little further. We have the faculty of insight, with which, as the word implies, we see within ourselves. Having observed the workings of our mind, we then externalize what we have observed by reproducing it in the outside world. The computer is a good example of this. The computer reflects our logical reasoning faculty. Before its invention, many man-hours were spent in doing what the computer can now do mechanically and quickly. We externalized a particular process of our mind. Having made it an automatic and external function we are left with a question: what next? Many machines have taken over our previous labors. What new potential does it release within the human psyche? What are we now going to choose? What is the new status quo a basis for in the future?

All thought starts with a formulation. A workable structure is then made which reproduces this formulation. We invent or discover a particular sequence of actions that will bring something about that we desired. Necessity becomes the mother of invention. We bring possibilities together in a sequence, which gives them a relationship in time and space. The latest example of this process of actualization is in genetic engineering. Sometimes we give no thought to the consequences arising from our inventions until it is too late. Whether or not one considers it a good thing, we are now able to select "desirable" genetic characteristics and, with the existence of sperm banks and the techniques of cloning, it is only a matter of time before the know-how will be used by someone, somewhere, to produce cloned humans with so-called perfect human characteristics. This will happen because of a shortsighted view of what the human race is. This is no longer a fantasy but a scientific technique. After all, if we can breed sheep that produce a specific substance in their milk, why can't we do the same with human beings?

SEERSHIP

This brings one to the recurrent problem of seership or prophecy, which is how much of what one has seen to reveal to the public. Those who prophesy can also bind their hearers to what has been seen. If a seer sees death surrounding a person, should she tell him? What are the consequences of such foresight? Prophets cannot necessarily see the consequences of their foresight, but the way in which it is initially formulated governs the development of events. In the seeing they should allow some potential to be realized in time. The discovery that the energy in a structure divided by its mass was a constant has bound scientific thought for the last ninety years. It has given birth to the atomic bomb, the nuclear bomb, the creation of atomic power generators and further consequences in the field of high-speed particles. This is a form of seership. The ability to see a new relationship (in this instance between energy and mass) produces manifold consequences. Many times in human history, our great men have said, "We now know all there is to know about the world we live in." There are scientists today who are sure that they are at the final frontier of knowledge of the origin of the universe. However, seers break through existing worldviews and new knowledge becomes available. Darwin with his theory of evolution discredited the literal truth of the Bible, even though he did not intend to. Newton's work became to a certain degree discredited by the work of Einstein. Einstein did not entirely intend it so. With the invention of the computer much human endeavor has lost its meaning. On the other hand, computers are able to perform endless repetitive tasks, and because of that we are beginning to see that random activity in the presence of some law creates beautiful fractal patterns.

The faculty in human beings that creates or discovers order (it doesn't much matter whether it is creation or discovery) enables us as a species to realize some of the potentialities of creation. "The Lord God took the man and put him in the Garden of Eden to dress and keep it": the words could also be translated, "The Lord God took the man and placed him in the enclosure of time and space to work there and keep it in order." This reading seems to give the human race a function that is a little broader than the usual reading of the text allows.

As Paul says in 1 Corinthians (quoted in the previous chapter), prophecy is one of the functions of man. If one sees, should one speak? Paul says one should speak out only under controlled conditions. He also separates the interpretative function from the prophetic; perhaps this can give us a clue to the possible relationship between seeing and speaking. However, the distinction between one who sees and one who speaks is perhaps more apparent than real. The prophets of the Old Testament certainly spoke out loud and clear as well as being seers. One has to suppose that the duty to speak out when necessary is inherent in the prophetic function. If the path men are treading is a dangerous one, should the seer warn them? But the danger might well be important for the further development of mankind. Who can tell? If we see only in part, the consequences can be seen only in part. The future of the human race is full of many possibilities, and some of those who have seen some of the possibilities have spoken.

In my youth, George Orwell's *1984* was a terrible warning. The year 1984 came and went. The book presented a possibility that has only partially been realized: it did not come about in the way Orwell envisaged it. However, he spoke and there were those who heard. Did the hearers then decide that this was indeed a path that was morally dangerous for the human race and do something about it so that full and dire consequences of the original vision did not come about? Who can tell?

This brings us to the next problem of seership. If a possibility has been seen, there is no need to put the knowledge into general circulation. Dropping a suggestion in the right ear at the right time, seemingly by accident, may bring about change in what seems to be a perfectly natural way. The Hebrew definition of wisdom as skillful action is relevant. The wise person does not cause trouble. After all, if there is a simple way to do something, why do it the long and complicated way? The wisest actions are those that achieve the most results with minimum disruption and effort.

In developing countries, one of the perennial problems is that the educated section of the population wants to run things. They consider that they are not fitted for a subordinate position and to accept such a post is to be in effect discarded. The result is a shortage of middle-level management, which is exactly where the need is the greatest. The world cannot be entirely composed of generals and privates, for who is then going to do the donkey work, arranging supplies and backup and so on? This also applies in the fields of ritual and seership. The seer may perceive a possibility, but unless there are those who can actually arrange matters so that what is seen can be put into a physical form, of what use was the seeing? In the field of ritual, we need seers, watchers, manipulators, and workers. The seers we have already talked about at some length; watchers are those who decide whether it is necessary for a ritual to be performed at all. They know the purpose for the ritual and act as a bridge between the seers and the manipulators. The manipulators do not really know the purpose of the ritual, but they devise the ritual and arrange what needs to be done. The workers perform the ritual and know how to do it. These four levels must be catered for in any ritual setting; otherwise you end up with the problems equivalent to those of developing countries.

For example, take the notion of the commune. To some it is a great idea, but there needs to be an acceptable division of roles; otherwise the commune collapses under the weight of those who see what should be done but don't want to do it themselves. In the tradition I was trained in, if you made a suggestion about how something could be done, that was usually the occasion for you to take on extra work. "Them that sees it, does it!" I can assure you that after a little experience in this method of allocating work, one becomes very careful about making suggestions! It is also a simple training for taking responsibility for what one sees and does. Sometimes suggestions have hidden faults and dangers, and this method does help to stop one from blaming someone else for not doing a job properly. If the suggestion is a good one, then you might find yourself stuck with a task that might take ten years to complete.

Not everyone can be a seer. It is, however, in the capabilities of most human beings to understand and to become wise. One only has to look at the older generation, the grandparents, who, if there has been a modicum of truth in their lives, have learned from their life experiences and exhibit a natural wisdom and understanding in situations where the younger ones are floundering. Seership, however, is more specialized. Can you train a person to be a seer? Let us take an analogy from life. The parachutist jumps out of an aircraft into empty space; the miner goes down into the bowels of the earth; the deep-sea diver into the depths of the ocean; the astronaut into deep space where there is no air and little in the way of gravity. What is common to these people is that they face death. Death is a close acquaintance. So also with the seer. The seer has to face death in the unknown. When one is dealing with matters that actually exist in the present or may have existed in the past, there are always clues to how one can proceed. But when dealing with possibilities that have not yet come into being, one is dealing with a level of creativity where one must be able to transcend the self-created structure of one's thoughts, feelings, and actions. This transcendence is the death the seer must live with so as to enter unknown worlds. Creativity is by definition *not* a repetition or even a reworking of the past. It certainly is not a shaking up of one's own kaleidoscope of images. It is bringing new possibilities into the world. It is true that "we build the shapes of the future upon the stones of the past," but this only means that to give practical form to a new idea, we must use things that have already been created. It was an enormous leap for mankind when the first bow was made. It was another enormous stride when the wheel was invented and put to practical use.

DISCIPLINE OF A SEER

The training of a seer is long and laborious. First, there must be the relevant faculty within the person. This faculty, which is no less than the ability to look into the unknown, must be nurtured and trained. The person has to be willing to give up his or her possessions, beliefs, and certainties and to go out into an unknown realm of obscure beginnings and possibilities. Here there are no certainties or known realities. One literally has to die to the world and its values in order to see new possibilities. This training or process is dangerous to the psyche because it removes from it the motivations that have brought it up in the world and have fed and nourished it. There is here a definite possibility of losing one's basis in the world as well as one's deep motivation. Seeing the foolish things that man has done, and may do in the future, could lead to a loss of faith. It could also lead to extreme arrogance. These are the traps that face the seer. Therefore the discipline is harsh and a certain ritual has to be developed to ensure moral sensitivity, a willingness to give up one's motivations and the strength to go beyond the known.

What the seer sees must also be capable of transmission into the world. This means that the seer must have the necessary training and means to articulate and pass on the vision. This is not as obvious as it seems. Words may not necessarily be the means. But as has already been pointed out, not all the possibilities seen should be transmitted: some could be absolutely disastrous to the species as a whole. For example, suppose in the realm of germ warfare we could cultivate some disease that would only affect enemies and would not touch our own nation or our allies: this would create enormous temptations. The phrase "to be tempted of the Devil" would have real meaning. So for safety's sake, such matters should be hedged about with safeguards.

What the seer sees should be judged and checked by someone of wisdom and understanding. The passing on of the vision should be a matter of discretion, and the actual seeing and speaking should be out of hearing of those who as yet have no discretion. Finally, it should be passed on for the love of mankind.

In the Kabbalistic tradition the safeguards involve ritual purity, which includes all forms of purity. In the Judaic line this tradition covers every aspect of behavior, so that the individual is separated from things judged unclean. There has to be purity of everything, from clothing and food onwards, and rituals are performed to maintain and reinforce a high level of purity. One does not have to go that far, but it is certainly one way of doing the job of protection.

Certain rituals have to be created to protect not only the seer, but also the hearers and the interpreters. At this point, it may be as well, if we can, to differentiate between the various rituals that aid that process.

Varieties of Protective Ritual

There are three main varieties of protective ritual: ceremonial ritual, ritual magic, and magic proper. In a ceremony, a distinct task with a specific end in view is undertaken. The ceremony itself is repeated at different times and in different places, but the various ritualistic elements that make up the ceremony remain the same. Not only does its distinctive task remain the same, but one could also say that the purpose is never to change or alter things. It is not concerned with the creation of new possibilities, but with the fulfillment of existing tasks. It celebrates what already exists and reinforces it. Here ritual is a sequence of actions that leads to the desired results almost independently of any level of awareness above the ordinary. If it changes the consciousness of the participants . . . well, that's all for the good, but that is not its aim. A straightforward example of a ceremonial ritual is the case of a civil marriage where there is always one result: if the ceremony proceeds without any hitches, then the two people end up married.

In ritual or ceremonial magic, the magician is concerned with bringing about a specific state of affairs and manipulates the necessary elements to produce the change. Here the purpose of the ritual is to alter and change existing things. Specific rituals are set up to do certain things, say, healing, haunting, punishment, or reward. Each will involve a different set of activities to bring about its desired end. The rituals provide the framework for the manipulation of the unseen worlds for the desired result. In other words, one performs certain rituals to bring oneself into a state that is suitable for starting — in this case to perform magic. The scope of what is desired is endless, but, unlike ceremonial ritual, ritual magic requires knowledge and ability from the participants.

Magic proper does not need to be formal. The most effective magic that I have observed was performed by a group of people who were sitting around in an ordinary room, in an odd assortment of chairs, wearing ordinary clothes and chattering as usual. Then they just stopped smoking, drinking tea, and chatting. The leader reminded them why they were there, checked the roles each was to fulfill and then, without apparent evocation or invocation, proceeded with the matter. To me, as an observer, the atmosphere in the room became electric. It felt as though danger was present. In the course of time, I happened to attend a seminar on a comparatively abstruse branch of morphology and — whether or not this was a coincidence — one of the speakers talked about the very matter that the magical group had attempted to bring into general consciousness. I am, of course, bound not to talk about the particular matter or the people. Secrecy is, after all, only another word for discretion.

This example also draws attention to the fact that ritual does not have to be external. It can be an internal process. In fact, this group of people had been trained for many years; they also met, dressed correctly with their proper insignia, and carried out their particular ritual with full formality and precision. Over the years, the ritual aspect can become internalized.

The principles of the magical process can be seen in a mundane activity such as cooking. To cook, you go to the kitchen — to a working space designed for a specific purpose. You enter a particular field of space where you behave in an appropriate way. It is almost as if the space itself, its layout and all the paraphernalia, force you to behave like a cook. Often you can be sitting comfortably in the living room, too tired to do anything, but on entering the kitchen you start your little rituals and, before you know it, you have finished cooking the meal. Everybody has their own little rituals for the kitchen. Some like to clean the surfaces before they begin, others like a mess with all the ingredients laid out before them, and so on. Before you start cooking you have to decide on your dish. This is then the purpose for all your activities. The preparation of the dish involves getting the right ingredients, combining them at appropriate times, using appropriate tools, applying the right type of heat or energy to transform the ingredients. And eventually you get your desired dish — which, once eaten, starts a further process of transformation which changes your physical state. Hunger is quelled and growth is possible. Certainly cooking is a ritual act. However, you also have to know how to cook and this makes it an act of will: it cannot be done on automatic (unlike the eating) and therefore is not a ceremony. The art of cooking can be seen as a magical act and indeed it is not far from magic itself, if you replace your material ingredients with unseen forces and are willing to be surprised at where or how the end product turns up!

RITUAL SPACE

Worship is ritual if it is carried out in a formal manner. In our personal lives, how do we worship? Is it a spontaneous inner act of remembering your God in the midst of ordinary life? How did you come to that point of remembrance? Was it an internal ritual or was it completely out of the blue? Or perhaps our personal worship consists of daily prayers, devotional readings, and meditation in a special corner of a room — acts that can be recognized as part of our daily ritual.

Worship at a personal level can take any form we choose, but at a communal level religious ritual must provide a frame for varying degrees of awareness on the part of the congregation. These different levels of awareness are catered for and can be seen in the physical form of a place of worship. In a Christian church, where the physical structure of the church often takes the shape of a cross, the point where the two arms intersect represents the point of mediation. This crossing is very much like a crossroads, which leads to different spaces with their own particular functions. To go beyond the crossing represents the entry into the religious life itself. The choir who sit beyond this point should be capable of actually praising and magnifying the Lord; it is not just a place where people sing (as it is all too often these days). Beyond the choir lies the high altar, where the priest officiates, and behind this rests the bishop's seat; the priest conveys the presence of the Lord through the intermediacy of the bishop in his capacity as a living embodiment of the apostolic line. A deacon officiates from the level of the crossing.

As a member of the congregation, when you walk through the door, you are at the foot of the cross. At the porch you would have been greeted by members of the church who, in handing you the prayer books, are symbolically instructing you in the ways of the Church. In the early Christian Church they were called "doorkeepers," and this was a recognized function within the Church. The doorkeepers would catechize members as to their beliefs. There is usually a bowl of ritually purified water just before you enter the body of the church to help you to start on the journey of the religious life. As you enter through the door you also enter the central symbol of Christianity, the cross. From the foot of the cross the path delineates the place of the congregation — on either side — and then there are the side chapels, which commemorate the saints. To receive the central sacrament of the Christian Church, the congregation must ascend to the level of the crossing, and the priest must descend to administer the rites. The religious ritual provides a framework for the care of people, the care of souls, and the guarding of the flock.

TIMESCALE

Ceremonial magic provides a framework for the manipulation of the unseen worlds in order to bring about some particular end, which may be momentary, medium-term, or long-term. Rituals concerned with short-term objectives vary considerably in their form and depend on the circumstances of the times. Medium-term activities require repetition of ritual forms on a regular basis for anything up to six months or a year. Long-term objectives require much more regular application and should be repeated exactly for many years.

Very long-term objectives may stretch over centuries, and the rituals may develop and grow — some being subject to the fashions of the times, others being faithfully repeated over hundreds of years by millions of people occupying the same physical space. Objectives with this long a timescale can find it very hard to accommodate change or incorporate values that become dominant later on. They have to find ways of changing without changing. What is required is a framework or system that will not vary with the passage of time, yet is capable of being understood afresh by each successive generation. Any framework that is incapable of incorporating temporary alterations is inconsistent with basic human principle. This may well be part of the problem for the Christian Church today.

Systems

No system or framework should lag behind the state of human knowledge at any given moment. If a system is outmoded, it fails. At the same time, if it is so successful that it forms an immovable factor in people's worldview, it can hinder and block the further development of human knowledge. Such a system should be capable of development by reformulation. This reformulation could manifest in new forms of rituals, if that is necessary. The new rituals can still preserve knowledge, but in a new form. If Britain became a presidential republic, then there would be no need for the great rituals of coronation, the state opening of Parliament, the speech from the throne, or the trooping of the colors. It may, however, take fifty or more troubled years for a nation to establish new forms of ritual that become accepted generally by the populace.

A framework or system that works for human beings must account for both the mass and the individual. It must include both the importance of mankind and its evident unimportance in the context of the universe as a whole. Such a framework should enable people to live together and yet allow them to retain their individual differences.

Some anthropologists have classified certain cultures as either "shame" or "guilt" cultures. In a culture that emphasizes "shame," the will of the mass is of prime importance and to "lose face" or importance in the eyes of others means losing self-respect. When the culture is based on "guilt," the individual is the focus and is responsible for judging the worth of his or her actions. A true ritual framework allows both mass and individual responsibility. In political terms, neither the view that the state is supreme nor the view that individual rights are paramount is a balanced view in itself.

Leaving such matters to one side, ritual sustains our life from our rising to our going to bed. Ritual is seen as imprisoning when we are in our teens, and as sustaining when we are older. The ways in which we relate to our fellow workers are governed by rituals, and the young who replace us learn these rituals as they begin to work with us. In the Middle Ages, the apprenticeship system accommodated these factors. Nowadays, with the rapid rate of change in our working lives, these little rituals have gone by the board. Because new types of labor require new ways of looking at things, most new tasks are performed by the young, with their up-to-date training. Because such tasks themselves change, there is very little continuity. Workers have to be more flexible, families more mobile, and relationships transient. The result is that we have no time to build up rituals. In time, perhaps, we may evolve the necessary rituals. The ways in which we do so will themselves illustrate the specialization-simplification-standardization process mentioned earlier.

Such rituals cannot evolve without a systematic framework. A framework based on natural principles can provide consistency in life, but not one which is just a set of laws that are expected to be obeyed. The set has to be self-consistent; it has to create a wholeness of itself with few internal contradictions, and any contradictions have to be accounted for and balanced out. In order for human beings to continue to live together, without having to invoke the power of nuclear weapons or any other fear mechanism, we will need to create a system that will enable Christian sects to meet with Jews, Jews with Arabs, Arabs with Indians, Indians with Chinese or Japanese, all upholding their own sets of religious beliefs.

At the time of this writing, a war is going on between two sects of Moslem believers, complicated by that salvation and disease of modern times, nationism. Nationism is not quite the same as nationalism. Nationalism implies geography, whereas nationism implies an identification of the people with the more abstract idea of a "nation"; this is where many current problems lie, rather than with identification with a geographical territory. There are rituals that uphold this abstract sense of nationhood. Each morning in the U.S., children at school salute the flag and "the republic for which it stands." This ritual is shared by all new Americans, and it is probably part of the cement that joins fifty separate regions into "one nation under God." Not so long ago in Britain our national anthem started and concluded all important meetings and public entertainments. The Welsh start their mass spectator games with song. Song and music are rituals in themselves.

What we know today beyond any doubt is that we are members of a family of mankind, that mankind is part of life on earth, and that mankind will one day go out into the galaxy and maybe even travel to the starry worlds beyond our galaxy. We know that whether or not we like it, we are affected in one way or another by what happens within the body of life on earth, and we know that our basic DNA structure is the same regardless of race, nation, color, language, belief, or religion. We also know that trying to eradicate a strain from the human race is a dangerous path to tread. If the war against Nazism taught us anything, it ought to have taught us that. Since the war, two major ritual forums have developed. One is the United Nations, whose authority is growing, but the extent of its operational powers has still to be tested. The other forum is the strange and peculiar aftereffect of the British Empire, the Commonwealth, and in particular the ritual meeting of the Commonwealth heads of state. A ritual forum it certainly is; whether it has any power we cannot be sure (though it certainly has influence), but it may be a seed from which a new human culture could evolve.

CHAPTER TEN

AN OLD NATION

You appoint your own ruler.

—Instructions to Members, Order of Sentinels

B RITAIN HAS A HISTORY OF NOT HAVING BEEN INVADED for a thousand years. So it has had the chance to grow in an organic fashion. Even the Normans in the eleventh century really only took over the upper echelons of society; the lower strata remained comparatively untouched. The Normans soon learned that the force of custom and tradition and regard for common law was so strong that if they contravened it, they would have no one left to rule over. One could say that Britain gained the upper hand and conquered the conquerors. Even the Romans seem to have been content to control only central matters of government rather than interfering at every level. Common law was recognized by nearly everyone and there were still large tracts of common land. According to the Domesday Book, Britain at this time was mainly wooded and it was very easy for the disaffected to disappear into the forests. This is the origin of the Robin Hood stories.

Such common law could not exist except by general agreement. Mechanisms existed already for dealing with problems, so Britain never went the way of France, with its monarchic despotism based on immutable law and the mystique of the Holy Blood. Since the Anglo-Saxon kingdoms came to power in about 850 A.D., methods had been evolved for handing over the authority to someone acceptable by most of the ruled. Rulership was originally elective, or at least required the acceptance of the tribal leaders; there was less chance, therefore, of familial dynasties becoming entrenched. Kingship was established as the most practical form of rulership and became accepted in common law by the compliance of the populace. Even the Norman William the Conqueror had some claim to the crown (though he was a bit impatient to wear it), and in due course he was anointed and crowned king of England.

At that time there was cooperation between Church and state. The Church had the authority to anoint the king, since that was a religious matter, and this anointing is still seen as the central act of coronation. Pagan customs were also assimilated into the process of the coronation, and some of the mystique monarchy still possesses is based on ancient rituals that lie too far back in British history to be traceable.

Coronation means "crowning." To be crowned is one thing; to be accepted by the people is something else again. So one of the most important aspects of the coronation ritual is the procession through the crowds of ordinary people by the monarch both before and after the ceremony. The procession before the coronation is to confirm that the right person is being crowned. In fact, this was crucial in days when the king was elected and succession was not by right of primogeniture. The election ceremony (a formal acclamation or election by the bishops and nobles) usually took place the day before the actual coronation in Westminster Hall. The monarch then would process from there to Westminster Abbey for the rites. This held real meaning: it was the opportunity for the people to discover who had been chosen and to approve the choice. The new heir is formally acclaimed immediately on the death of the king or queen at St. James's Palace. The coronation ritual itself starts with the formal recognition of the new monarch. But the procession is still the means whereby the people offer their implicit recognition. The procession after the crowning is for the people to see for themselves that the right person has been duly appointed.

The monarch exercises power and authority in both the spiritual and temporal realms. If the people have given their consent to the new monarch before the ceremony, and within the ceremony their worldly and spiritual leaders have also given their consent and have handed over the symbols of authority to the new monarch, then they know who their ruler is and they tacitly accept his or her authority. In earlier times, the anointing meant that the king's person had been transformed into something sacred. Perhaps this belief had sprung up from an earlier past when the king was looked upon as combined magician, priest, and god. In Christian times the act of kingmaking was a sacramental rite, and it is interesting to note that it has to this day never been fundamentally altered. Whatever the fashionable climate may be, it is still a fact that England is a Christian state with a religious foundation and the ruler has to be inaugurated with Christian rites.

State ritual is the framework within which power is exercised. From the ritual of the dissolution of Parliament to the election of a new government, from the state opening of Parliament to the Lord Mayor's Show, from budget day to the prime minister's question time in the House of Commons, all is governed by ritual. The ritual of the coronation is worth studying in some detail, as it embodies many of the formal and informal relationships that have evolved among the peoples of Britain.

The Coronation of a Monarch

The Parliamentary Acts of Succession (of which there have been many) established all the rules for descent of the monarchy, so that even if an unforeseen disaster on a large scale (such as nuclear war) were to occur, there would always be somebody, however remote, in the line of succession. So the death of one monarch automatically means the accession of another, male or female. "The king is dead, long live the king."

As has already been pointed out, although accession is immediate, coronation is not. On the death of a monarch the wheels start turning. Invitations to the coronation have to be sent out to all the heads of state. How many people can Westminster Abbey hold? How much media coverage is to be allowed? How big should the delegations be and where should they each be accommodated? Soldiers, airmen, sailors, police have to be organized. Orders of precedence have to be consulted, traditions checked, all interested parties given their say (and there are a lot of interested parties!). If there is to be a spectacle, then it had better be effective!

Think of all the arrangements it takes just to organize the processional route. The local authorities will be involved in closing off streets and rerouting traffic. This requires signposting and decorating the roads with the correct notices and flags. The armed forces and police will line the route. High security measures are to be taken to ensure against terrorism. There is order to be maintained among the people thronging the whole length of the processional route.

The proceedings for the day start early, as it takes a few hours for all the guests to fill up the Abbey. They enter in strict order of precedence. First the guests, followed by the minor royals (that is, those not directly of the blood royal), followed by foreign representatives, the heads of all the states in the world in strict order of diplomatic precedence. Then come the representatives of the Church, and the deans and prebendaries of the Abbey who carry the royal regalia for the ceremony.

THE ROBES AND REGALIA

The coronation robes are worn only on this occasion in the monarch's lifetime. Both the robes and the regalia reflect the spiritual and temporal authority and power with which the monarch is vested. The robes that represent spiritual authority are very similar to a bishop's garments, which suggests that their origin lies in the time when anointing was believed to confer priestly status on the monarch.

The *Colobium Sindonis* is a long white sleeveless linen robe (rather like the alb worn by a bishop when he is celebrating Mass); it is open at the side, edged all round with lace, and gathered in at the waist by a linen girdle. The *Dalmatic* is made of cloth-of-gold lined with rose-colored silk; it has short wide sleeves and is decorated with palm leaves, pink roses, green shamrocks, and purple thistles. The *Stole* is again made of cloth-of-gold lined with rose-colored silk. At either end of its five-foot length is the red cross of St. George on a silver background. In the Church it is worn as an emblem of authority, and bishops wear it round the neck hanging down in front, uncrossed, whereas priests wear it crossed while celebrating Mass. At the coronation it is worn over the Dalmatic. The *Pall* or *Imperial Mantle*, made of cloth-of-gold (with rose-colored silk lining), is worked in a pattern of silver coronets, fleurs de lys, green leaves, shamrocks, purple thistles, and silver eagles. It is very similar to a bishop's cope except that it is not rounded at the bottom but has four corners to represent the four corners of empire. It is the final robe to be placed on the newly consecrated monarch.

The *Imperial Robe* of royal purple is worn after the coronation for the procession out of the Abbey; it is made of purple velvet, lined and edged with miniver and ermine tails; it is hooded and has a long gold-embroidered train. The *Crimson Robe of State* is worn in the procession to the Abbey before the coronation. It is made of crimson velvet embellished with gold lace; it is lined and edged with miniver and has a long train. It is also the robe worn for state openings of Parliament. The *Cap of Maintenance* is worn by a male sovereign on his progress to the Abbey, while it is carried before a queen regnant. It is made of crimson velvet lined and edged with miniver. This or another cap of maintenance is carried before a monarch by a peer on a short baton at the opening of Parliament.

So much for the robes. The royal regalia consist of those emblems with which the sovereign is actually invested at the coronation. The *ring* is a sapphire and ruby cross of St. George set in fine gold; this signifies the wedding of the monarch with the people and that the monarch is the "Defender of Christ's Religion." The *Armills* are two bracelets representing sincerity and wisdom; each is made of solid gold and together they symbolize the bonds that unite the monarch with the people. The *Golden Spurs* (also known as St. George's Spurs) are of solid gold with gold-embroidered crimson velvet straps. They represent knight-hood and chivalry, and in medieval times the bestowal of spurs formed an essential part of the making of a knight. The *Jeweled Sword of State* is the most magnificent of the swords carried at the coronation; both hilt and scabbard are elaborately decorated with gold tracing and precious stones. *St. Edward's Crown* has four fleur-de-lys and four crosses around the rim; arches link the four crosses and there is an orb and a cross at the point of intersection. *St. Edward's Staff* is made of gold but has a steel tip; it is four feet, seven and a half inches long. It is carried before the monarch in the procession to the Abbey to guide his or her steps. The *Royal Scepter with Cross* is the ultimate symbol of kingly authority. It is made of gold and has mounted beneath the cross the largest portion of the Cullinan diamond, weighing five hundred carats. The *Scepter* or *Rod with Dove* is also made of gold but is surmounted by a gold and white enamel dove signifying the Holy Spirit. It is delivered as the rod of equity and mercy.

The next two symbols — the *Orb with Cross* and the *Second Crown* — are highly significant, although strictly speaking they are not part of the actual regalia for the ritual of kingmaking. The Orb with Cross is a golden ball surmounted by a heavily jeweled metal band from which springs a jeweled arch with a cross at the apex. It became part of the coronation rite comparatively late. It is presented before the delivery of the Royal Scepters and again for the procession out of the Abbey. The Second Crown was always worn by the monarchs on important occasions and is today worn at the state opening of Parliament. This crown, also called the Imperial State Crown, was made for Queen Victoria's coronation. Set with many historic gems, it is more splendidly jeweled than St. Edward's Crown.

The nobles and officers of the Church also have their own sets of regalia for a coronation. The symbols of coronation associated with the sacramental aspect of the rite are handled by the clergy alone. These include the chalice and paten without which no Eucharist can be celebrated. Two of the most historically interesting items of the regalia are the *Ampulla* and the *Anointing Spoon*, which are thought to be the actual vessels used in medieval coronations. The

Ampulla is a hollow vessel of solid gold in the form of an eagle; it holds six ounces of oil, which is poured through the beak. The spoon is of silver gilt and is probably older than the Ampulla. It is used by the archbishop to convey the sacred oil to the various parts of the monarch's body.

There are four swords that are carried by the nobles and form part of their regalia. The largest of these is the two-handled Sword of State. It represents the power of the state itself and today is the only one of the four seen outside a coronation, since it is carried before the monarch at the state opening of Parliament. There are two *Swords of Justice*, one representing spiritual power and the other temporal justice. The fourth sword is called the *Curtana* because it has a blunted end: it is a symbol of mercy.

ENTER THE MONARCH ELECT

All the regalia have been placed in the Abbey. Now the monarch enters the Abbey, clothed in the Crimson Robe and Cap of Maintenance and proceeds to pray privately. Then the Archbishop together with the Lord Chancellor, Lord Great Chamberlain, Lord High Constable, and Earl Marshal present the monarch to the four quarters — east, south, west, and north — asking all to recognize the true monarch and to pay homage. With trumpets and loud acclamations of "God save the King (or Queen)," the ceremony proceeds to the Litany, when all the regalia (except the swords of the nobles) are placed on the altar. We then start the communion service and after the homily the monarch takes the Coronation Oath. With Bible in hand, he promises to govern the people, to execute law and justice in mercy, and to maintain the laws of God.

EMPOWERMENT

The monarch is disrobed of the Crimson Robe and the Cap of Maintenance. While the Archbishop is blessing the oil, the monarch sits on the Chair of Edward. This is built around the Stone of Destiny from Scone Abbey in Scotland. The Scottish kings used to be crowned on it until Edward I took it from them in 1296. Ever since, it has been used for the crowning of English monarchs. The monarch sits on the Stone of Destiny, under a canopy of cloth-of-gold which is held by four Knights of the Garter. The Archbishop then proceeds to anoint the monarch with the Holy Oil taken from the Ampulla using the Spoon. The monarch is anointed first on the crown of the head "as kings, priests, and prophets were anointed," then on the breast and the palms of both hands. The palms represent the physical, the breast symbolizes the heart, and the crown of the head represents the intellect. The oil is a symbol of grace and benevolence. It impresses the gift of the Holy Spirit. In times past monarchs were also anointed in the middle of the shoulders, the shoulders themselves, and the inside of the elbows. This was symbolic of the wings of the spirit. Unfortunately this is no longer done. This part of the service is the actual empowering of the monarch and is accompanied by the words: "And as Solomon was anointed King by Zadok the priest and Nathan the prophet, so be you anointed, blessed, and consecrated King/Queen over this People, whom the Lord your God hath given you to rule and govern, in the name of the Father, and of the Son, and of the Holy Ghost."

Then the canopy is taken away and the monarch is dressed in the vestments of a bishop with the Colobium Sindonis, the Dalmatic, the Pall, and a girdle. Thus robed, the Golden Spurs are presented. The custom now is to touch the king's heel with the spurs, but they used to be buckled on. A queen only touches them. The spurs signify that the monarch is head of all orders of knighthood. The Jeweled Sword of State is next given to the monarch (a king will gird the sword, while a queen touches it only) and is described as a "kingly" sword with which to "restore, maintain, reform, and confirm" order. The sword is then taken by a peer and redeemed for a "hundred shillings," and drawn out of the scabbard and carried naked in front of the monarch for the rest of the ceremony. The monarch is then invested with the Bracelets of Sincerity and Wisdom and the Pall or Imperial Mantle. The monarch has now been established as the nation's priest or priestess.

CONFIRMATION

Now begins the investiture of the monarch, dressed in the Robe of Righteousness, with earthly power. He or she receives the Orb with these words: "And when you see this Orb thus set under the Cross, remember that the whole world is subject to the power and empire of Christ, our Redeemer." Next the monarch is wedded to the spirit of the land with a ring. The Orb is laid aside, and the monarch is given the Scepter with the Cross, the ensign of royal power and justice, to hold in his right hand, and the Scepter with the Dove, the Rod of Equity and Mercy, for the left hand. Now the monarch is crowned by the Archbishop with St. Edward's Crown and everybody shouts "God save the Queen/King." The Peers and Kings of Arms all put on their coronets, trumpets sound, and the guns in the Tower of London fire their salute.

The clergy then present the monarch with the Holy Bible, signifying wisdom, and bless him or her. The monarch leaves King Edward's chair and goes to the throne, which is lifted up by the clergy and the peers, the officers and nobles. This is a relic of an ancient rite in which the king was raised on his shield above the people so that all could see. All the relevant persons present pay public homage. Individuals from the clergy, royals, and peers come up to the monarch, swear fealty and allegiance, and kiss the monarch's cheek. After this the monarch descends from the throne and goes to the altar where the Crown, Scepter, and Rod are delivered to the Lord Chamberlain. The monarch offers the bread and wine for communion to the Archbishop, and also makes an offering to the abbey of an altar cloth and a gold ingot. The service continues, and when the bread and wine have been administered to the monarch, he or she puts on the Crown and takes up the Scepter and Rod again. At the end of the service the monarch retires to be disrobed and puts on the Royal Robe of Purple Velvet and the Imperial Crown. He or she takes the Orb in his left hand and the Scepter with the Cross in his right hand for the long procession in the state coach back to the palace, through the waiting and cheering crowds. Once at the palace, the monarch must make a statutory appearance on the balcony to wave again to the crowds.

RECOGNITIONS

When people assemble in procession in large numbers, the spectators are affected by colors and by feeling. If the paraders are all dressed in different colors and clothing, there is plenty of stimulation for the eyes and ears, but, as with Brownian movement, there is no order in it. When there is no order, there is excitement but no satisfaction. Each new stimulus starts off a train of associations in the perceiver and is replaced by another train, but there is no connection between the two. There is nothing for the feelings or the mind to rest upon. On the other hand, if there is order in the procession, with uniforms and bands and cavalry and coaches, robes and coronets, there is sufficient difference for the eye not to be bored. There is a theme running through the parade. The feelings can cohere, the mind perceives order, continuity is established. Unconsciously one is reassured: there is order in the world. The coronation is a drama wherein the order of the state is publicly enacted. Rightly or wrongly, the spectator feels that things are all right, that someone is looking after the state.

Although Hitler and other fascist dictators ensured that their public rituals were massive, they did not imbue the rituals with enough fun and enjoyment. They impressed strangers with the danger of the situation, not with delight; they were not the summation of centuries of different experiences. All state displays are an enactment of the structure of the society. Those states that consider all their members as being basically the same tend towards mass displays of gymnastics, weaponry, and sheer weight of uniformity. For me, the spectacle of ten thousand people all performing the same actions on some great celebration is terrifying. I feel that the people have been reduced to worker ants. But so be it. No doubt that is how that particular state is happy to perceive itself.

As for the coronation, the whole procedure evokes in the mind of the British people their history and the continuity of the nation. It invokes the aid of God and Christ, and the monarch, the clergy and peers, all the guests and the crowds participate in these events. The coronation itself provides a ritual of defense. The armed forces are represented by their senior officers. It commemorates the monarch by the historic allusions and the age of some of the items involved. It initiates a reign: it shows that a new beginning has been made. It empowers, in that the symbols of monarchy are bestowed; and the handing over of the weapons acknowledges mastery. The monarch is confirmed in status when he is placed on the throne and acclaimed by the clergy, peers, and people. Becoming a monarch means giving up a private life. It may not have been so drastic in the days before television and radio, but now it certainly is so. Even Edward VIII found that he was forced to abdicate because of his private life.

It is not easy to relate and know with certainty the result or consequences of any one action. How can we possibly judge the consequences of the great ritual act of Queen Elizabeth II's coronation? Was it a successful ritual? History will judge the political, philosophical, and social results.

Afterword

One who knows cannot speak.
One who speaks cannot know.

—Instructions to Members, Order of Sentinels

Do rituals work? Amusingly, there are one or two rituals in most people's lives, one of which is about 90 percent effective and the other of which is about 99 percent effective. The first is the naming ritual at the beginning of one's life, and the second is the funeral at the end of one's life. One establishes the name and the other remembers it.

If we apply practical tests to see how effective rituals are, we would have to admit that the rituals of life are not 100 percent effective. The ritual in a high court does not always establish the truth of the case. The ritual of communion does not always have any effect on the conscious life of the participant. The rituals of baptism and confirmation do not always result in a Christian way of life. It has been argued both within and outside the Church that neither of these rituals should be carried out unless the person concerned can make those commitments knowingly.

The ritual of marriage is more of a social institution and a social commitment and as such is in the nature of a contract. Judging by contractual law standards, this ritual is not very effective. If you take on a fifty-year mortgage, you remain responsible for repayments for the full length of time, unless you manage to sell the mortgage! This has been found a problem with marriage, so the ritual of divorce has been established. Divorce, except in the Roman Catholic

Church, is rarely a religious matter; it is more a device of the state, required by the people. Perhaps marriage should no longer be a lifelong affair and we should replace the vow of "so long as ye both shall live" with a fixed period of years. This way the vow that is taken is entered into fully, unlike the situation nowadays, when the commitment made in the ritual act of marriage is halfhearted with an underlying knowledge of the growing social license that this "permanent" state of affairs need not be so at all.

Socially divorce is more and more acceptable, but the problems created by it are yet to be resolved. Children of broken marriages do suffer, however we gloss over the cracks. Despite that, what is emerging is a new "extended" family when divorcees bring to a new marriage the children of a former marriage. Stepparents and stepchildren may well be the new familial ties that we are creating, and if so, then perhaps it is best we lose the fairy stories that always have wicked stepmothers.

What has happened is that individuals and their desires have become of greater importance than values dictated by religion. Nevertheless individuals still require the approval of the society in which they live. If a laissez-faire situation exists, then it is the collective that has recognized the need and allowed the situation to carry on without interference.

DISCRIMINATION

With the increasing number of people living at close quarters in cities, the opportunities for interference from others are greater, and the occasions for temptations to arise and for us to give in to them are multiplied. The advent of mass media into the home itself means that the outside world intrudes more and more into private life, and until one can make a decision to censor the input, one is at the mercy of clamoring voices. Censoring what we take in is really the beginning of discrimination. Some people would say this is a deliberate turning away from the reality of what is happening and a blindness to truth. But you only need to see cruelty once to know what it is. If you keep harping on the subject, that may be a form of indulgence. Life is full of temptation, and perhaps we should try to cut down the opportunities for courting disaster and living on a razor's edge.

When a person belongs to a species that is not preprogrammed by instinct, then methods of meeting the unknown must continually be evolved. As the unknown is met with and mastered, patterns build up and the person becomes more and more bound by his past. This can result in leading a completely programmed life. If the outer circumstances change, a severe breakdown can occur when the programming fails to cope with the change. It seems that human beings, once they cease to take in new information and organize it, begin the long journey down into the grave. They are living on their capital.

To recapitulate, we know that we can live on what one could call a purely animal level, and at this level a sense of "I" is hardly necessary. Survival as a living organism is the only goal; instinct rules. At the next plateau of existence, it is necessary to acknowledge other human beings as living beings in their own right. Children who have been institutionalized from birth with next to no human interchange do not seem to develop a flexible sense of "I." Human feelings seem to be at a very low level of activity in them. Another effect of this lack of stimulation is that their intelligence often operates at a low level. Whether this is due to a lack of suitably learned rituals or a lack of language is a moot point. Learning a vocabulary for sensory experience certainly seems to be necessary in order to flower as a human being.

The next level of operation is the ability to oversee our own operations, in that we are able to detach from what is happening and view ourselves almost as though we were standing aside and letting ourselves carry on with whatever we are doing. This faculty or level of operation has the ability to step into the picture and almost, as it were, wake us up to the importance of what is happening. This faculty is called the "watchman," and its activity is the one the disciples were asked to undertake when Jesus told them to "watch and pray" in the Garden of Gethsemane. This faculty takes notice not only of what is happening in the external world, but also of our sense of being, around which all else revolves.

THE PLAYER ON THE OTHER SIDE

This sense of being has been described as "the player on the other side." In the physical layout of a cathedral, the position of the bishop as shepherd of the flock is symbolic of this sense of being. It is that within us that moves us around the gameboard of life, and brings us inevitably to the one situation we have always feared. If we look back on our life as a sequence of actions, we can sometimes see that although we had many opportunities to choose differently, we did not do so. What choices we made we would probably make all over again in the same way and for the same reasons. P. D. Ouspensky's novel *Strange Life of Ivan Osokin* illustrates this point hauntingly: the hero is given the chance to live his life all over again so that he can choose a different path, but he forgets he has a choice and repeats the same decisions and the same apparent mistakes. It is this "player on the other side" that persists. Sometimes, though very rarely, we become conscious of this real being within us. This being has self-knowledge.

We need rituals for our "I." These are our daily rituals, such as shaving for a man, putting on makeup for a woman. Dressing in a particular manner for a particular task is another such ritual, as are arriving at work, departing from work, talking, and exchanging gossip. These rituals form the framework for all the different activities of the "I." They all make its operation easier, requiring little in the way of conscious activity. At another level, however, we have personal rituals by which we take stock of our many differing identities. We need to access that within us that perceives the meaning of life. Some meditate, some fall into a reverie before a fire, some watch the waves on the sea. Others look at the clouds, lie on the beach, or gaze at the wonders of nature. Whatever they do, they become aware of the watchman or sentinel at the doors of the mind. This is the faculty that is able to discern sense in what is happening. When it happens, everyday matters are seen as of no particular importance.

Lastly — and this is the real aiming point for most people who are interested in the magical — there is the encounter with death. Here one's own self-importance is sacrificed on the altar of the Creative. It is as though the screen of the forehead is flooded with cool and fragrant oil. At such times one is not afraid to gaze upon the nothingness within, because one knows that it is the source of all within us that is worthwhile. Some call it faith, "the evidence of things unseen." One cannot call it belief because it has no object. Only the other operations of mind require objects, words, or images. Some call it knowledge, but again it is knowledge itself, not knowledge of anything in particular. It is not death, though it may be the gate of death. It is certainly life, but it is not *my* life.

DEATH SHALL HAVE NO DOMINION

To meet death without fear is to encounter the Creative within. But one's ordinary mind runs screaming from the encounter back into a world that is familiar, frantically piling explanation upon explanation and reasoning the experience away as fast as possible. To come to terms with this experience, most (though not all) people require a map and a framework that make it acceptable to the ordinary mind. It is not easy to know that one has created one's life from the beginning. Practicing the approach in a ritual manner with signposts of experience on the way helps our normal "I" to come to terms with the existence within us of that which is greater than we can normally conceive. Clearing a space, making the weapons, empowerment, evocation, and invocation bring us to the purpose of human life. To quote from *The Essence of Plotinus* by Grace Turnbull: "What then is the achieved sage? One whose act is determined by that higher phase of the Soul. . . . With this spirit it embarks in the skiff of the Universe. The spindle of necessity then takes control and appoints the seat for the voyage. The seat of the lot in life . . . this it is that constitutes Destiny."

As you can see
there are 12 of them.
If you can find any more,
it will be a big
surprise.

INDEX

acupuncture, 22
age of responsibility rituals, 17–18
aggression rituals, 14–15
air, 36, 126
Aladdin, 70
alchemy, 34, 42
alienation, 155–56
allegiance rituals, 19
alphabet, 64–65, 71–73
American rituals, 15–16, 19, 178
amulets, 74
angels, 24, 39, 163
animals
  identification with, 151–52
  instinctiveness of, 162
  responses to danger and
    unknown, 159–60
  rituals, 13–14, 15
  survival in animal kingdom, 159
animism, 22
anointing, 182
appearance/disappearance, 35–36
appearances, 40, 129, 131–33
apprentice rituals, 99–100
apprenticeship, 99–102, 104–6, 107,
  109, 177
Aquarius, 56
archangels, 39
archetypes, 24, 39
arguments, 152
Aries, 55, 60
Armenians, survival of, 159
Armstrong, Neil, 76
art, as mankind-level dreams, 154
assessing significance, 136
association, chains of, 136, 137
astral travel, 155
astrology, 54–56
atomic energy, 165
attentiveness, 84–85, 86
awareness, 135, 174

Babylonian and Assyrian Religion
  (Hooke), 47–48
Babylonian ritual, 47–49
bad influences, defending against,
  69–70

Baha'ullah, 154
balance, 22, 84, 109–10
baptism, 17, 25, 28, 195
bark, 83
bar mitzvah, 18
Bastille Day, 19
being, 136–37, 198
belief, 74
Billy Liar, 153
biosphere, venturing into, 22–23
birth rituals, 16
black-handled knife, significance of,
  68, 98
Book of the Art of Dying (Dalton),
  138
Book of Changes, 56–57
bow, 87
bowl, 95
breathing, 83
British history, 181
British rituals, 12–13, 15–16, 19,
  178
Broda (Lord of Necessity), 45
Buddha, 20, 30, 154
Buddhism, 19, 20, 21, 78

calendar, 20–21
Cancer, 55
Capricorn, 55–56
caste system, 21
catechism, 69, 175
Catholicism, 26
celestial phenomena, 19
ceremonial magic, 171, 172, 175–76
ceremonial ritual, 171–72
Ceres, 39
change, sensitivity to, 152
chanting, 24
charged (holy) water, 23, 24, 37–38,
  175
charging, 26
Charles, Prince of Wales, 75–76
charm bracelets, 69
Chernobyl, 129
child naming rituals, 16–17, 195
choice, 198
Chomsky, Noam, 66